BORN TO WIN

WILLIAM MacDONALD

EMMAUS
INTERNATIONAL

Developed as a study course by Emmaus Correspondence School, founded in 1942.

Our vision is to see hearts and lives transformed for Christ through the study of God's Word.

Born to Win

William MacDonald

Published by:
Emmaus International
PO Box 1028
Dubuque, IA 52004-1028
phone: (563) 585-2070
email: info@emmausinternational.com
website: EmmausInternational.com

First Edition 1977 (AK '77), 1 Unit
Reprinted 2006 (AK '90), 1 Unit
Revised 2008 (AK '08), 1 Unit
Reprinted 2009 (AK '08), 1 Unit
Revised 2012 (AK '12), 1 Unit
Reprinted 2013 (AK '12), 1 Unit
Revised 2015 (AK '15), 1 Unit
Reprinted 2016 (AK '15), 1 Unit
Revised 2018 (AK '18), 1 Unit

ISBN 978-0-940293-15-1

Code: BTW

Printed in the United States of America

COURSE OVERVIEW

We are glad that you are interested in studying the Bible. Our Bible courses provide an excellent introduction to the Bible and will lead you, one step at a time, through many of its great truths (salvation, Christian growth, Bible book studies, doctrine, topical, Bible survey, etc.). Feel free to complete these courses at your own pace and your own schedule.

The Bible pictures losers in many ways—as lost sheep, mug victims, lower class citizens, frauds, and runaway kids, to mention just a few. But the Bible also contains the good news that God has provided a way to have a fresh start in life. Do you feel like you're a "born loser"? This Bible course will help you learn how you can be born (again) to win! Someone has expressed it this way:

There's a way back to God from the dark paths of sin,
There's a door that is open and you may go in.
At Calvary's cross is where you begin,
When you come as a sinner to Jesus.
–E. H. Swinstead

Lessons You Will Study

STUDENT INSTRUCTIONS

This Emmaus course is designed for people seeking to know God and desiring to receive Bible training. In order to complete the course, you will need access to a Bible. Before you begin each chapter, it is a good practice to read the Bible passages prayerfully. Ask God to reveal His truths to you, and help you understand its message.

Course Content

In order to help you understand the Bible, this course has three parts: the *lesson content,* the *exam questions*, and an *answer sheet* (included at the end of the course) for you to record your answers to the exam questions.

Lesson Content

Each lesson is written to help explain principles and truths from the Bible. Read each lesson (or chapter) through at least twice—once to get a general idea of its content, and then again, slowly, looking up any Bible references given. It is important that you read the Bible passages referenced as some questions in the exams may be based on the Bible text.

Passages in the Bible are listed by book, chapter, and verse. For instance, 2 Peter 1:21 refers to the second book of Peter, chapter 1, and verse 21. At the beginning of every Bible there is a table of contents which lists the names of the books of the Bible, and tells the page number on which each book begins. Look up 2 Peter in the table of contents and turn to the page listed; then find the chapter and verse.

Exam Questions

At the end of each lesson, there is an exam, which is designed to check your knowledge of the course material and the Bible passages. After you have studied a chapter, review the exam questions for that lesson. If you have difficulty answering the questions, re-read the chapter. You are permitted to look up any answers of which you are in doubt, and you are encouraged to use your Bible to help you answer them.

It is best *not* to answer the questions based on what you think or have always believed. The questions are designed to find out if you understand the material in the course and the Bible.

What Do You Say?

These questions are designed for your personal reflection, and to help you express your ideas and feelings as you process how to apply the content of each lesson to your life.

Answer Sheet

Use the exam questions to complete the answer sheet included at the end of the course. The exams contain multiple choice questions. When you have determined the right answer to a question, fill in the corresponding letter on the answer sheet.

Write It Out!

The answer sheet also contains one or two *Write It Out!* questions. These questions are included to help you write out what you have learned in this course. While they will not be counted as part of your grade, they will be reviewed and responded to by your Emmaus Connector.

Talk to Us

You may include your personal comments on the exam sheet. They help us to get to know you and your needs better. Please let us know specific questions you may have about the Bible, God, or other spiritual matters.

Submitting the Answer Sheet

When you have answered all the exam questions on the answer sheet, check them carefully. Slowly tear out the answer sheet along the perforated edge provided near the course spine.

Fill in your contact information and submit it to your Emmaus Connector or the organization from which you received it.

Returning Your Exam Sheet

Please tear out the exam sheet and give it to your Emmaus Connector or MAIL it to the address listed here.

EXAMS TO: JOHN PLASTERER
BCDC CHAPLAIN'S OFFICE
OR MAIL TO
BALTO SCHOOL OF BIBLE
1712 PARK AVE BALT MD 21217

If you're unsure of where to return your exam sheet:

MAIL the exam sheet to

Emmaus International
PO Box 1028
Dubuque, IA 52004-1028

OR

EMAIL a scan or photo

of both sides of the exam sheet
to this email address:

Exams@EmmausInternational.com

Taking Your Exam Online

By receiving this printed course, you automatically have access to the online eCourse. If you'd prefer to take your exam online, visit the product page for this course:

emmausecourses.com/courses/born-to-win

Click the "buy" button, and during checkout, enter the following coupon code:

46r8-nd27-9yf6-67tr

This code will give you immediate access to the eCourse and online exam. **This code is for *your use only*; do not share.**

Your Results

A passing grade is considered at least a 70% average score on your exam. After finishing this course, you will be awarded a certificate of completion.

CHAPTER

1

THE LOST SHEEP

Now the tax collectors and sinners were all drawing near to hear him. And the Pharisees and the scribes grumbled, saying, "This man receives sinners and eats with them." So he told them this parable: "What man of you, having a hundred sheep, if he has lost one of them, does not leave the ninety-nine in the open country, and go after the one that is lost, until he finds it? And when he has found it, he lays it on his shoulders, rejoicing. And when he comes home, he calls together his friends and his neighbors, saying to them, 'Rejoice with me, for I have found my sheep that was lost.' Just so, I tell you, there will be more joy in heaven over one sinner who repents than over ninety-nine righteous persons who need no repentance.

–Luke 15:1-7

This is one of the best-loved stories of the Christian faith—the story of the lost sheep. It is about a shepherd who had a flock of one hundred sheep. One day one of them wandered off and became thoroughly lost. What should the shepherd do? Should he be satisfied that he still had ninety-nine sheep left? No! He left the ninety-nine and searched tirelessly until he found the missing one. Then he put it on his shoulders and went home happy and triumphant. As soon as he arrived, he called his friends together and said, "Rejoice with me, for I have found my sheep that was lost."

When Jesus told the story, He had two classes of people in mind. There were the tax collectors and sinners—people who knew they were "lost." And there were the Pharisees (the strictest of the Jewish sects) and scribes (writers, and interpreters of Jewish laws) who would never confess to being sinners. The one sheep that went astray represents the tax collectors and sinners. The ninety-nine sheep picture the Pharisees and scribes who were never broken before God and never admitted that they were away from

God and in a "lost" condition. The fact was, they were as lost as the tax-collectors and sinners, but they refused to admit it.

Jesus used the story to teach that there is more joy in heaven over one sinner who repents than over ninety-nine self-righteous persons who refuse to admit their need to repent.

We can apply the story to ourselves. We are like the sheep that wandered away. That sheep was pretty stupid and dumb. It was lost, helpless, in danger, and it couldn't find its own way back. Isaiah, the Old Testament prophet, was right when he said, "All we like sheep have gone astray; we have turned—every one—to his own way" (Isaiah 53:6). And the apostle Peter reminds us also that we are like sheep going astray (1 Peter 2:25). Jesus, of course, is the Shepherd. He is the Good Shepherd (John 10:11), the Great Shepherd (Hebrews 13:20) and the Chief Shepherd (1 Peter 5:4). Let's notice the close parallels between Jesus and the shepherd who went after the lost sheep.

Jesus is the Good Shepherd, the Great Shepherd, and the Chief Shepherd.

Love Is More Than a Song

First of all, Jesus loved us. Long before we ever knew Him, He loved us. Before the foundation of the world, He loved us. No one ever loved us like He did.

His love made Him leave His home in heaven. He really didn't have to come here. He was living in perfect happiness with God the Father. Nothing ever entered heaven to upset or disturb Him. There was nothing He needed to make His rest and peace more complete. But because He knew that there were lost sheep like us on earth, He left heaven above.

His love made Him come down to this world of sin. We can't imagine what a tremendous step down it was for the Son of God to come to earth and to be born as a baby in a stable in Bethlehem. We can't realize what it meant for the absolutely Holy One to live in a world of sin and rottenness. We can't conceive what it cost Him who was so rich to become so poor!

Then, like the shepherd in the story, He went out searching for the lost sheep. He said, "the Son of Man came to seek and to save the lost" (Luke 19:10). Men rejected Him, but still He kept seeking. The religious leaders persecuted Him, but still He kept seeking. Even His friends forsook Him, but still He kept seeking. He would not be discouraged. He would not turn back. He would not give up. He was determined to "find" the sheep.

The shepherd's love led Him to give His life for the sheep, as He said, "I am the good shepherd. The good shepherd lays down his life for the sheep" (John 10:11). This was most unusual. Ordinarily the sheep have to die for the shepherd, that is, he sells them to the meat packer so he can get money. But the Good Shepherd died for the sheep. On the cross of Calvary, the Lord Jesus died to save us from our sins. He died to pay the penalty that our sins deserved. He died so that He could bring us to God. None of us will ever know what He had to suffer in order to seek the sheep that was lost.

How to Get a Pardon

Now, the shepherd sends out the good news to all the world. If any guilty, lost sinner will repent of his sins and receive Jesus Christ as his Lord and Savior, that person gets saved. His sins are forgiven. He receives eternal life as a free gift (Romans 6:23). That's when the Savior finds us—when we cry out to Him, "Lord, save me!"

We see the shepherd putting the rescued sheep on his shoulders. The shoulders, in the Bible, speak of strength. What a beautiful picture this is! It reminds us that our Shepherd is able not only to save us, but to keep us too. The Savior said, "My sheep hear my voice, and I know them, and they follow me. I give them eternal life, and they will never perish, and no one will snatch them out of my hand. My Father, who has given them to me, is greater than all, and no one is able to snatch them out of the Father's hand" (John 10:27-29).

No one ever loved us like Jesus did.

The shepherd never stops till he brings the lost sheep safely home. And our Shepherd will never stop until He has brought all of His sheep safely home to heaven. It gives great happiness to His heart every time one of His loved ones lands safely on the other side!

Years ago, Israel's King David wrote a beautiful tribute to the Good Shepherd. We know it as the twenty-third Psalm. It goes like this:

> "The Lord is my shepherd; I shall not want.
> He makes me lie down in green pastures.
> He leads me beside still waters.
> He restores my soul.

He leads me in paths of righteousness for his name's sake.
Even though I walk through the valley of the shadow of death,
I will fear no evil, for you are with me;
Your rod and your staff, they comfort me.
You prepare a table before me in the presence of my enemies;
You anoint my head with oil; my cup overflows.
Surely goodness and mercy shall follow me all the days of my life,
And I shall dwell in the house of the LORD forever."

In this Psalm we have:

1. The secret of a happy life—"The LORD is my shepherd." There are many people who say, "The LORD is *a* shepherd." Others say, "The LORD is *the* shepherd." But that isn't enough. We must be able to say from the heart, "The LORD is *my* shepherd."
2. The secret of a happy death—"Even though I walk through the valley of the shadow of death, I will fear no evil, for you are with me." When a man's sins are unconfessed and unforgiven, he is afraid to die. But the believer isn't afraid to meet God, because he knows that his sins are gone. And he does not fear death because he knows Jesus will be with him and take him safely through the valley.
3. The secret of a happy eternity—"Surely goodness and mercy shall follow me all the days of my life, and I shall dwell in the house of the LORD forever." The future is safe and sure for the child of God. He is certain of a home in heaven. The Shepherd has promised it, and He can never go back on His promise.

CHAPTER 1 EXAM

Use the exam answer sheet at the back of the book to complete your exam.

1. **Who wrote, "All we like sheep have gone astray"?**
   A. Moses
   B. Isaiah
   C. Luke

2. **Jesus left His home in heaven because**
   A. He loved us.
   B. He was unhappy there.
   C. He was restless and dissatisfied.

3. **Why did the Good Shepherd die?**
   A. Because He was a martyr
   B. Because He couldn't escape
   C. So that He might save us from our sins

4. **After we're saved, the Savior tells us**
   A. "Hold on or you may be lost again."
   B. "I give you eternal life and you'll never perish."
   C. "I've done my part—now you get the rest of the way to heaven on your own."

5. **The secret of a happy death is**
   A. having lived a long life.
   B. having lived a productive life.
   C. knowing that your sins are forgiven.

6. **The writer of the beloved Shepherd Psalm (23rd) is**
   A. Moses.
   B. David.
   C. Isaiah.

7. **The secret of a happy life is to be able to say with truth "the LORD is**
   A. a shepherd."
   B. the shepherd."
   C. my shepherd."

8. **According to Luke 15:7, where is there rejoicing over the lost sheep (sinner) being found and saved?**
   A. Among the Pharisees
   B. Among the 99 already in the fold
   C. In heaven

9. **When we repent and receive Jesus as our Savior**
   A. we get religion.
   B. we get saved.
   C. we start on the road toward salvation.

10. **According to Romans 6:23, eternal life is**
   A. partly earned and partly a gift of God.
   B. earned by good works such as church attendance.
   C. entirely a free gift of God.

What Do You Say?

Are you lost or are you saved? How do you know?

CHAPTER

2

THE GOOD SAMARITAN

Jesus replied, "A man was going down from Jerusalem to Jericho, and he fell among robbers, who stripped him and beat him and departed, leaving him half dead. Now by chance a priest was going down that road, and when he saw him he passed by on the other side. So likewise a Levite, when he came to the place and saw him, passed by on the other side. But a Samaritan, as he journeyed, came to where he was, and when he saw him, he had compassion. He went to him and bound up his wounds, pouring on oil and wine. Then he set him on his own animal and brought him to an inn and took care of him. And the next day he took out two denarii and gave them to the innkeeper, saying, 'Take care of him, and whatever more you spend, I will repay you when I come back.' Which of these three, do you think, proved to be a neighbor to the man who fell among the robbers?" He said, "The one who showed him mercy." And Jesus said to him, "You go, and do likewise."

–Luke 10:30-37

It was a dangerous stretch of road between Jerusalem and Jericho, crawling as it was with bandits. But it was the only practical route between the two cities, so what could a person do but take the chance?

One day, a Jewish fellow was walking down this desert highway when a gang jumped out from the bushes and mugged him. The most valuable things he had were his clothes, so they took them, and left him bleeding and half-conscious.

After a while, a Jewish priest came along and saw the victim (one of his own church members) lying in the powdery dust. Normally the priest would have liked to help him, but his own life was at risk out there in the wilds. Every moment of delay would only increase his own danger. So he hurried by on the other side of the road.

The next passer-by was a Levite. Also a Jew, his job was to assist the priests at the temple. He noticed the robbery victim, who was obviously in need of first-aid. But then it might be a trap! Maybe if he stopped to help, some thugs would jump him. So he kept on going.

Finally, a Samaritan came along on his donkey. The Samaritans were half-breeds that Jews looked on with prejudice and contempt. Normally, the Jews and Samaritans had nothing to do with each other. But when this particular Samaritan saw this Jew in distress, he moved into action. Forgetting racial prejudices as well as his own safety, he knelt down, cleaned the wounds, put medication on them, and bandaged them. Then he lifted the man onto his donkey and took him to the nearest inn. That night he continued to take care of the man as best he could.

In the morning, the Samaritan had to leave. But he gave money to the innkeeper and asked him to take care of this Jew until he was ready to travel again. And if the money wasn't enough, he promised to pay the balance on his return trip.

Say what you want, it was pretty decent of the Samaritan to do what he did—especially to show such mercy to a Jew, when there were such bad feelings between the two races.

Get the Big Picture

Now when Jesus told a story like this, He always had some definite lesson to teach. In this case He had been teaching a lawyer that a man should love God with all his heart and that he should love his neighbor as himself. The lawyer didn't like that. It made him feel uncomfortable. So he tried to turn attention away from himself by asking Jesus, "Who is my neighbor?" Jesus answered the question by telling the story of the Good Samaritan. The answer is this: our neighbor is any fellow human being who needs our help, no matter his race, creed, or color.

We believe however that the story also gives us an excellent picture of how the Lord Jesus shows mercy to those who are in desperate need. Let's go back over the story and see how it resembles the gospel, the good news of salvation.

First of all, this fellow started down the road from Jerusalem to Jericho. Jerusalem means "the city of peace." Jericho is located by the Jordan River which flows southward into the Dead Sea. So the picture is of a man was traveling downhill from the city of peace to the place of death. That reminds us that "there is a way that seems right to a man, but its end is the way to death" (Proverbs 14:12).

In his downward journey, he fell among thieves. It is true of us too that when we turn our backs on God and start downhill, we run into trouble. The Bible says, "the way of the treacherous is their ruin" (Proverbs 13:15). Sin has built-in consequences which are impossible to escape.

The thugs robbed this poor guy, and sin is like that. It robs people of being clean, having joy, being free, and everything else that is worthwhile in life. The robbers also wounded him and left him half-dead. This is a vivid reminder of the heartache, the misery, the guilt, the scars, the regrets that sin brings into human lives. And pay-day is sure to come, "for the wages of sin is death" (Romans 6:23).

You Can't Cop a Plea

The priest and the Levite passed by; they didn't stop to help. This suggests several lessons. First, man can't be counted on to help the sinner in his need; "The help of man is useless" (Psalm 60:11 NKJV). Second, even religious leaders—preachers, priests, or rabbis—cannot save the soul. Only the Lord can do this. Third, if we view the priest and the Levite as representing the law (because it was the law of Moses that appointed them), then the lesson is that the law—specifically, the Ten Commandments—cannot save. God gave the Ten Commandments to *show* men and women that they are sinners, not to save them. The law is like a mirror. It shows a man that his face is dirty, but it neither can nor will wash his face for him.

We see several similarities between the Samaritan and the Lord Jesus Christ. We should first explain, however, that Jesus was not a Samaritan by birth. He was a Jew. However, His own people despised and rejected Him *as if* He were a Samaritan. At one time, they actually called Him a Samaritan, "are we not right in saying that you are a Samaritan and have a demon" (John 8:48), a kind of racial put-down.

Like the Samaritan, Jesus came to us in our desperate need. He came all the way from heaven to this jungle of sin in order to seek and save those who were lost. Like the good Samaritan, Jesus showed wonderful mercy and grace. It was really very kind of a despised Samaritan to be so helpful to a Jew who was in need. But it was even more kind of the Lord of life and glory to suffer, bleed, and die for a world of ungodly sinners. The apostle Paul expressed the wonder of it when he wrote: "For you know the grace of our Lord Jesus Christ, that though he was rich, yet for your sake he became poor, so that you by his poverty might become rich" (2 Corinthians 8:9). Jesus became poor to make us spiritually rich.

The Man Who Didn't Duck Out

The Samaritan risked his life by stopping to help the robbery victim. Jesus not only risked His life—He actually gave His life for us. "The Son of God, who loved me and gave himself for me" (Galatians 2:20).

The Samaritan bound up the wounds of the victim lying on the road. The Lord Jesus does even better. He heals the broken hearted and gives sight to those who are spiritually blind (Luke 4:18). The oil which the Samaritan poured onto the man's wounds is a picture of the Holy Spirit, given to all when they are saved by God. The wine pictures the joy in the Christian life. The Savior pours oil and wine into the life that has been wounded by sin.

The Samaritan didn't leave his new friend stretched out on the highway. He brought him to an inn. So the Lord leads those who are saved into the warmth and fellowship of other believers, especially in the local church. If we were left alone, we would be in constant danger of falling into sin. But through the fellowship of other Christians, we are strengthened to live clean and straight.

Before leaving the inn, the Samaritan took care of all the needs of his new friend until he would come back again. And so does Jesus. He gave us His Word, the Bible. He gave us His Holy Spirit. He gave us the church, with its teaching, its fellowship, its prayer meetings, and the Lord's Supper. He gives us strength for each day and the promise that He will come again and take us to be with Himself so that we will be with Him forever.

And so the story of the Good Samaritan gives us a beautiful and accurate picture of what the Savior has done for us in our deep need. The story presents three philosophies in the world today.

- "What's yours is mine, and I am going to get it." This was the philosophy of the gangsters.
- "What's mine is my own and I am going to keep it." This was the philosophy of the priest and the Levite.
- "What's mine is yours and I want you to share it." This was the philosophy of the Good Samaritan.

CHAPTER 2 EXAM

Use the exam answer sheet at the back of the book to complete your exam.

1. **The story of the Good Samaritan**
   A. is a beautiful picture of what Christ has done for us.
   B. has nothing to teach us today.
   C. proves Jesus was really a Samaritan.

2. **Jesus told this story in order to**
   A. make the lawyer feel good.
   B. please the people.
   C. teach us to love both God and other people.

3. **The road from Jerusalem to Jericho was**
   A. uphill all the way.
   B. downward all the way.
   C. well-traveled and safe.

4. **All the miseries suffered by the wounded man best picture**
   A. the results of sin.
   B. poor medical conditions in those days.
   C. cruelty of bandits and criminals in general.

5. **God gave the Ten Commandments to**
   A. save us from sin.
   B. help us earn our way to heaven.
   C. show us that we're sinners.

6. **Galatians 2:20 shows that, like the Good Samaritan, the Lord Jesus**
   A. gave Himself for me.
   B. will only help religious people.
   C. saves chiefly through teaching the Ten Commandments.

7. **Oil in the Bible is a picture of**
   A. the joy of Christian life.
   B. the Holy Spirit.
   C. Middle East petroleum wealth.

8. Jesus gives to the genuine believer in Him

A. deliverance from sickness.
B. eternal life.
C. anything he wants.

9. The Bible tells us that sin

A. doesn't matter.
B. brings consequences that we can't escape.
C. makes us happy and free.

10. The philosophy of the Good Samaritan was

A. "I'm keeping what's mine."
B. "I'm going to take what's yours."
C. "I'll share what I have with you."

What Do You Say?

What is your philosophy of life—to keep, to take, or to share? Would your choice please God?

CHAPTER

3

THE PHARISEE AND THE TAX COLLECTOR

He also told this parable to some who trusted in themselves that they were righteous, and treated others with contempt: "Two men went up into the temple to pray, one a Pharisee and the other a tax collector. The Pharisee, standing by himself, prayed thus: 'God, I thank you that I am not like other men, extortioners, unjust, adulterers, or even like this tax collector. I fast twice a week; I give tithes of all that I get.' But the tax collector, standing far off, would not even lift up his eyes to heaven, but beat his breast, saying, 'God, be merciful to me, a sinner!' I tell you, this man went down to his house justified, rather than the other. For everyone who exalts himself will be humbled, but the one who humbles himself will be exalted."

–Luke 18:9-14

First of all, let's get the meaning of these two words clear—*Pharisee* and *tax collector.* A Pharisee was a member of a religious sect that prided itself in its strict observance of the law of God. But the Pharisees became so concerned about small details that they neglected the great duties of life. And because they didn't practice what they preached, they became known as religious phonies.

A tax collector was a man who collected taxes for the Roman government. The tax collectors mentioned in the Gospels were Jews, and because these Jews worked for the Roman oppressor, they were despised by the other Jews as traitors. They also had a reputation for skimming money for themselves. Therefore, they were practically excluded from religious activities.

Well, anyway, a Pharisee and a tax collector went up to the temple to pray. The Pharisee probably stood in a very obvious place and prayed loud enough for others to hear. What he said was something like this: "God, I'm really proud that I'm not as bad as a lot of people I know—such as that low-down tax collector over there. I am not cheating people. I don't work for our enemies. I don't commit adultery. I go without eating twice a week and put money in the offering plate regularly. I know that I'm okay with You."

The tax collector found a place in the shadows where he would not be seen. He felt so no-good that he would not even look up to God. Instead, he beat his chest, being really down on himself, and prayed, "God, be merciful to me, a sinner."

Jesus gave the meaning of the story. He said that the tax collector was the one who got right with God because he took a low place. The Pharisee went back home as guilty as ever, because he boasted about himself before God.

Let us look at these two men and their prayers, and see which one we are like.

Two Ways of Talking with God

The prayer of the Pharisee was all about himself. He used the personal pronoun "I" five times. He was a real "I" specialist. He bragged about what he did and what he didn't do. He went without eating twice a week, whereas the law required it only once a year (Leviticus 16:29; 23:27, 29; Numbers 29:7). He gave a tenth of all his income, whereas the law required only a tenth of corn, wine, oil and cattle (Deuteronomy 14:22-23).

The prayer of the tax collector was lowly. He stood afar off, as if he were unclean and, therefore, unfit to draw near. By beating his chest, he showed that he was putting self down, not making himself out to be an all-right guy.

The Pharisee compared himself with others: "I am not like other men . . . or even like this tax collector." When we do this, we can always find others who are worse than we are.

The tax collector compared himself with God's standard, that is, the law, and he realized how guilty and no-good he was. The Ten Commandments are like a straight line. It is only when we put ourselves next to that straight line that we realize how crooked we are. We can put ourselves next to God's standard by answering "Yes" or "No" to the following questions:

- Do you love God with all your heart, soul, mind, and strength? (see Mark 12:30)
- Do you love your neighbor as yourself? (see Mark 12:31)
- Have you honored your father and mother as you know you should? (see Exodus 20:12)
- Has your thought life always been clean? (see Mark 7:21-23)
- Have you ever looked at a woman with lust in your heart? (see Matthew 5:28)
- Have you done all the good you know you should have done? (see James 4:17)
- Have you ever stolen? (see Exodus 20:15)
- Have you ever told a lie? (see Exodus 20:16)
- Have you ever killed anyone? (see Exodus 20:13)
- Have you ever used the Name of God in profanity or as a curse? (see Exodus 20:7)

The Right Way and the Wrong

The tax collector did not look to others. He judged himself by God's standard and realized he was a guilty sinner.

The Pharisee was depending completely on himself and on his own works. The tax collector was depending completely on God's mercy.

The Pharisee was boasting on how good he had acted. The tax collector was throwing himself on the mercy of God's court.

The Pharisee talked as if he were the only saint: "I am not like other men." In contrast, the tax collector acknowledged that he was a guilty sinner.

The Pharisee felt self-sufficient. He didn't need anything or anyone outside himself. The tax collector realized he needed someone else to make an offering that would satisfy God. He needed a substitute. When he prayed, "God, be merciful to me," he was saying, in effect: "I know that I can't make it right for my sins, so I ask You to provide a sacrifice that will provide a satisfactory basis for forgiving my sins." We know that God has provided such a sacrifice. He sent His Son to die for our sins. Death is the penalty for all sins (Romans 6:23). Jesus died in our place. When we receive Him as Lord and Savior, God can be merciful to us and can forgive our sins, because the penalty has been paid.

You Don't Get If You Don't Ask

So we see that the tax collector asked for mercy and got it. The Pharisee, on the other hand, asked for nothing, and that's what he got.

The one who refused to repent went away guilty. The one who admitted his need was justified. This simply means that he received a right standing before God. God justifies—counts as righteous—all those who come to Him as confessed sinners, who believe that the Lord Jesus Christ died for their sins, and who receive Him as their Lord and Savior by a definite act of faith. God can't forgive anyone until first that person says, "I have sinned."

There is one final contrast between these two men. The Pharisee honored himself and was put down. The tax collector put himself down and, as a result, was honored as an example of repentance.

There is a sense in which these two men represent the only two religions in the world. Someone may object that there are hundreds of religions in the world—Buddhism, Hinduism, Judaism, Christianity, and many more. Yes, but basically there are only two. The Pharisee represents all those religions which teach that man earns his own salvation, at least in part. They say he is saved by doing right, by being religious, by giving money, by being good, and by doing the best he can. Of course, he can never know he is saved as long as he is on earth, because he doesn't know if he has done enough good works or the right kind of works.

The tax collector represents the *true* religion. This teaches that man cannot save himself. But it also teaches that God provides salvation as a free gift to all who take their place as sinners and who receive the Lord Jesus as their only hope for heaven.

The Pharisee's religion can be summed up in the word, "*Works.*"

The Pharisee sings:

> Every day in every way
> I'm getting better and better.

The tax collector sings:

> In my hand no price I bring,
> Simply to Thy cross I cling;
> Naked, come to Thee for dress,
> Helpless, look to Thee for grace.
> Foul, I to the fountain fly;
> Wash me, Savior, or I die.

CHAPTER 3 EXAM

Use the exam answer sheet at the back of the book to complete your exam.

1. **"Every day in every way, I'm getting better and better" was the philosophy of**
   A. the tax collector.
   B. the Pharisee.
   C. the religion of grace.

2. **Religious Pharisees tried to get right with God by**
   A. faith alone.
   B. self-righteous religious practices.
   C. accepting the teachings of Jesus.

3. **The tax collectors mentioned in the Gospels**
   A. were not Jews.
   B. worked for Rome.
   C. were honest and upright men.

4. **We should be like the tax collector and depend on**
   A. God's mercy.
   B. God's mercy and our own best efforts.
   C. church membership and Holy Communion.

5. **The prayer of the Pharisee**
   A. was all about himself.
   B. exalted God.
   C. praised other men.

6. **The tax collector knew that**
   A. God would not hear his prayer.
   B. God would not forgive a sinner like himself.
   C. God was merciful and would forgive a repentant sinner.

7. **The tax collector put himself down and was**
   A. disgraced for all time.
   B. honored by being exalted as an example of repentance.
   C. never able to look people in the face again.

8. This story shows us that

A. those who try to live right will be saved.
B. God is happy to hear any kind of prayer.
C. those who cry out for God's mercy are blessed by Him.

9. The great sin that is so common and is illustrated by the Pharisee is

A. pride, or self-righteousness.
B. cheating the taxman.
C. majoring on minor issues.

10. The true religion teaches that

A. the church alone can save us.
B. we can earn our own salvation.
C. God provides salvation as a gift to those who receive the Lord Jesus.

What Do You Say?

On what do you base your hope of salvation and heaven?

____

____

____

____

CHAPTER

4

THE REBEL COMES HOME

And he said, "There was a man who had two sons. And the younger of them said to his father, 'Father, give me the share of property that is coming to me.' And he divided his property between them. Not many days later, the younger son gathered all he had and took a journey into a far country, and there he squandered his property in reckless living. And when he had spent everything, a severe famine arose in that country, and he began to be in need. So he went and hired himself out to one of the citizens of that country, who sent him into his fields to feed pigs. And he was longing to be fed with the pods that the pigs ate, and no one gave him anything.

"But when he came to himself, he said, 'How many of my father's hired servants have more than enough bread, but I perish here with hunger! I will arise and go to my father, and I will say to him, "Father, I have sinned against heaven and before you. I am no longer worthy to be called your son. Treat me as one of your hired servants."' And he arose and came to his father. But while he was still a long way off, his father saw him and felt compassion, and ran and embraced him and kissed him. And the son said to him, 'Father, I have sinned against heaven and before you. I am no longer worthy to be called your son.' But the father said to his servants, 'Bring quickly the best robe, and put it on him, and put a ring on his hand, and shoes on his feet. And bring the fattened calf and kill it, and let us eat and celebrate. For this my son was dead, and is alive again; he was lost, and is found.' And they began to celebrate.

"Now his older son was in the field, and as he came and drew near to the house, he heard music and dancing. And he called one of the servants and asked what these things meant. And he said to him, 'Your brother has come, and your father has killed the fattened calf, because he has received him back safe and sound.' But he was angry and refused to go in. His father came out

and entreated him, but he answered his father, 'Look, these many years I have served you, and I never disobeyed your command, yet you never gave me a young goat, that I might celebrate with my friends. But when this son of yours came, who has devoured your property with prostitutes, you killed the fattened calf for him!' And he said to him, 'Son, you are always with me, and all that is mine is yours. It was fitting to celebrate and be glad, for this your brother was dead, and is alive; he was lost, and is found.'"

–Luke 15:11-32

It was an emotion-packed moment in the house that day. The younger of two sons decided that he had had it. He was leaving home—for good. Only one problem: he didn't have any money. His father had all the money. Sure, when his father died, he'd get a third of it, but that didn't do him any good right now.

Rather coldly, he asked his dad, "How about giving me my share of the family fortune—like now?"

For a minute the father looked hurt—as if he had been stabbed—but then, surprisingly enough, he gave his son all he asked for. As soon as he got it, he took off for Sin City.

Man, it was great! No more nagging. No more generation gap. Freedom at last from the old man's bossing around. Lots of good shows. Eating and drinking. Doping and gambling. Everybody was his friend, especially the chicks who saw how cool he really was. He spent that money like it was going out of style. (That's where he gets the name "prodigal." Prodigal means wasteful.) Night after night, he picked up the tab for his friends in fancy night spots. "Last of the big-time spenders," they kidded.

Then the roof fell in—just as his money was running out. Unemployment. High prices. Food shortages. Past-due bills piled up.

From Big Spender to Pig Feeder

Man, this dude was hungry, but his friends had split when the money ran out. When he wanted a drink, no one would set him up. And now that he couldn't pay his rent, he was thrown out on the street.

At last he got a job offer—big deal, feeding pigs! Good thing his priest couldn't see him now, feeding dirty swine. But he envied those pigs. Their bellies were full; his was empty.

As he stood by the stinking pig-pen, he often thought of home: of the family sitting at the well-decked table, of the smell of freshly baked bread, and of the servants—why, they were better off than he was! He was starving! What a fool he'd been!

Finally, he broke. He'd go back to his father, apologize for being such a fool, and ask for forgiveness.

The father must have been waiting for him, because he saw him way down the road. Leaping up from his chair on the porch, the father ran down to meet him. The prodigal son began to sob out his confession, but he was interrupted by the father's hugs and kisses. What a welcome! No put downs! No suggestion of, "I told you so." Just love, man, just love!

As soon as they got back to the house, the father had the servants running in every direction—now for a suit, now for a gold ring, now for new shoes. Then they began preparing a feast—roast veal and all the fixin's.

"My son was dead and is alive again; he was lost and is found."

The father was bubbling over—beside himself with joy. He said, "My son was dead and is alive again; he was lost and is found." And the celebration went on into the night.

When the older son came home from work and found out what all the celebration was about, he blew his stack. The father asked him why he wasn't joining in on the festivities. He whined, "I never left home. I never took off for Sin City. I never wasted your money on chicks. But did you ever make a feast like this for me? You never even roasted a young goat for me, to say nothing of a calf. Never. Your son there has been good-for-nothing, and you throw a party when he comes home. I've been decent and respectful all the time, and what do I get? Nothing!"

The father answered him kindly, but what the answer boiled down to was this: there is more reason to rejoice over a bad-news son who confesses his sins and comes home than over a holier-than-thou type who thinks he has no faults.

The Meaning of the Story

Jesus told this story to self-righteous people who criticized Him for being a friend of sinners (see Luke 15:2). The father in the story stands for God. The younger son pictures the sinner who is willing to repent and seek forgiveness. The older son is also a sinner, but he's not willing to admit it. He compares himself with others and thinks he's doing okay. The main point of the story is that God gets joy over the sinner who repents, but He gets no joy over the unbroken, unrepentant sinner who is always bragging about his good works and his innocence.

But there are other lessons in the story that we don't want to miss.

It must have broken the father's heart when the younger son wanted to leave home and asked for his inheritance. So sin is not only breaking God's law, it's breaking His heart.

The younger son went to a far country and sowed his wild oats. Most of us do the same. We want to taste what the world has to offer, to enjoy the pleasures of sin. We have to learn as he did that the pleasures of sin are short-lived, that they don't provide lasting satisfaction.

When we have nowhere else to turn to, we can always look up.

As long as his money held out, he had lots of friends. But they ditched him when he really needed them. No one gave to him. Someone has said, "In the Devil's country, nothing is given; everything must be bought at a terrible price."

The hard times of the famine were a blessing in disguise. It often takes a tragedy, an accident, a sickness, a sorrow, or some serious crisis like that to bring us to our senses.

The only work the fellow could find was feeding pigs. It was very degrading, a real bummer. Sin is like that. It brings a man way down.

Finally, in his distress, he came to himself. It was an opening for God—man's extremity is God's opportunity. When we have nowhere else to turn to, we can always look up.

No doubt his father had been praying all the time he was gone. Prayer changes things. It changes people too. Many of us can say, "My mother's (or father's) prayers have followed me."

The son left home saying, "*Give* me my share." He came back saying, "*Make* me your servant." In other words, he left asking for what he felt he deserved. He returned asking for grace and mercy. Grace is better than justice.

The father's welcome gives us a tremendous picture of the heart of God. This is about the only place in the Bible where hurry is used of God in a good sense—when He runs out to welcome the returning sinner.

The best robe pictures the suit of righteousness in which God dresses the sinner when he repents and puts his faith in Christ (see 2 Corinthians 5:21). The shoes show that believers are not brought into God's family as slaves, but as heirs. Slaves did not wear shoes.

In describing the welcome-home celebration, the Bible says they began to be merry. It doesn't say they ever stopped! When a sinner comes back to the Father, the joy never ends.

A Modern Prodigal

Some years ago, a young fellow left his home in this country and started to live it up in another state. He really blew it. For ten years he brought shame and disgrace on his parents. Then, like the prodigal, he decided to go home and make things right. But would his folks receive him back? He wasn't sure.

So he wrote a note, telling of his plan, and asking his mother to tie a strip of white cloth on the lilac bush out front if it was okay for him to come home. When the Greyhound bus passed the house, he would know the answer. If there was no white cloth, he would keep on going.

When the bus finally did pull in to his hometown, he tensed up. Finally, the old homestead came into view. The lilac bush was there, completely covered with hundreds of strips of torn sheeting, waving lightly in the breeze. He got up from his seat and made his way to the front of the bus to get off. He knew that he was welcome home.

That's the way it is with God too. He has a tree out front—the Cross of Calvary. His arms are outstretched to sinners everywhere, urging them to repent and turn from their sins and to embrace the sinner's Savior.

CHAPTER 4 EXAM

Use the exam answer sheet at the back of the book to complete your exam.

1. **The younger son asked his father for**
   A. money that belonged to his brother.
   B. his share of the family wealth.
   C. advice on how to use money.

2. **While he was away from home, the prodigal learned that**
   A. his friends loved him for himself, not his money.
   B. he could take care of himself very well, even in hard times.
   C. he was a fool to leave home.

3. **"Man's extremity (very bad situation) is God's ___________."**
   A. opportunity
   B. lost cause
   C. chance to condemn as soon as He can

4. **This story illustrates that**
   A. God has favorites.
   B. God wants to give us material wealth.
   C. God gets joy over the sinner who repents.

5. **Sin is not only breaking God's law, it's**
   A. different in different religions.
   B. breaking God's heart.
   C. asking God for mercy.

6. **When his younger son confessed his sin, his father**
   A. made him a servant in the home.
   B. welcomed him and dressed him as his son.
   C. sent him away in disgrace.

7. **The older son's reaction to his brother's repenting was**
   A. great joy to see junior restored to the family's good graces.
   B. a keen desire to get along with him.
   C. to get angry.

8. The older son was

A. wrong in his attitude to his brother.
B. lazy and careless.
C. glad that his father forgave his brother.

9. God treats repentant sinners

A. harshly, with punishment.
B. coldly, with indifference.
C. lovingly, with forgiveness, as the father did the prodigal.

10. The white cloths in the lilac bush in the modern story of the prodigal son illustrate

A. how foolish and sentimental old people can get.
B. full and free forgiveness.
C. wastefulness of good sheets.

What Do You Say?

Which one best pictures you—the self-righteous older brother or the repentant prodigal?

CHAPTER

5

THE BAD SCENE THAT TOPS THEM ALL

"There was a rich man who was clothed in purple and fine linen and who feasted sumptuously every day. And at his gate was laid a poor man named Lazarus, covered with sores, who desired to be fed with what fell from the rich man's table. Moreover, even the dogs came and licked his sores. The poor man died and was carried by the angels to Abraham's side. The rich man also died and was buried, and in Hades, being in torment, he lifted up his eyes and saw Abraham far off and Lazarus at his side. And he called out, 'Father Abraham, have mercy on me, and send Lazarus to dip the end of his finger in water and cool my tongue, for I am in anguish in this flame.' But Abraham said, 'Child, remember that you in your lifetime received your good things, and Lazarus in like manner bad things; but now he is comforted here, and you are in anguish. And besides all this, between us and you a great chasm has been fixed, in order that those who would pass from here to you may not be able, and none may cross from there to us.' And he said, 'Then I beg you, father, to send him to my father's house— for I have five brothers—so that he may warn them, lest they also come into this place of torment.' But Abraham said, 'They have Moses and the Prophets; let them hear them.' And he said, 'No, father Abraham, but if someone goes to them from the dead, they will repent.' He said to him, 'If they do not hear Moses and the Prophets, neither will they be convinced if someone should rise from the dead.'"

–Luke 16:19-31

What do you think happens to a person when he dies? Most people have a keen desire to know, and that is why the story of the rich man and Lazarus grabs our interest. Here, in brief, is the story.

First we are introduced to this rich man. He wore the most expensive suits, ate the finest gourmet foods, and in general lived high off the hog.

Whenever he took the time to pull back the drapes on his living room window, he could see a pathetic sight down at the front gate. It was Lazarus, a poor beggar, who depended on hand-outs of food from others. Poor Lazarus was covered with sores that sometimes oozed with blood and pus. The neighborhood dogs used to come and lick his sores, and Lazarus probably didn't have enough strength to chase them away.

There was something you couldn't tell by looking at these two men, namely, that the rich man had never trusted in God but that Lazarus was a true believer.

Well, Lazarus died, and his body was buried. It wasn't a fancy funeral, you can be sure of that. Perhaps the county gave him a poor man's burial. But we read that the angels carried him (that is, his spirit and soul) to Abraham's bosom. When the Jews of that day used the expression, "Abraham's bosom," they meant the most wonderful state of happiness they could think of—in other words, heaven. They knew that Abraham had died and had gone to heaven; therefore, to rest on Abraham's bosom meant to enjoy heaven with Abraham.

How Is Your Lay-Away Plan?

The rich man eventually died and was also buried. You can fill in the details—expensive casket, lots of flowers, and a long sermon telling all the good things he had done—like sending his old clothes to the Salvation Army, or saving his used tea bags for the poor. But he didn't go to Abraham's bosom; the Bible says that he was in Hades, in torment. Hades is a place of conscious suffering where the unsaved go at the time of death. They remain there until the final resurrection when their bodies will be raised and reunited with their spirits and souls, and will be sent to hell (which is also called the lake of fire). Hades is like a county jail where a person waits until he is sentenced. Hell is like the state prison or federal penitentiary where he serves his sentence.

In Hades, the rich man could see across a great chasm and see Abraham and Lazarus. He cried out, "Father Abraham, have mercy on me, and send Lazarus to dip the end of his finger in water and cool my tongue, for I am in aguish in this flame."

The request was not granted. Abraham reminded him that in life he was able to get anything he wanted, while Lazarus got a lot of trouble. But now the tables were turned. In addition, Abraham pointed out that the great chasm could not be crossed either way. The rich man then began to think of his five brothers who were still living. He asked Abraham to send Lazarus to them and warn them so that they wouldn't ever have to come to Hades.

Abraham reminded him that his brothers had the sacred Scriptures written by Moses and the prophets. If they would read them, they would learn the way of salvation through faith in the Lord.

The rich man didn't think this was enough. But he was sure that if someone went to his brothers from the dead, they would believe.

Getting in the Last Word

Abraham had the final word. He pointed out that if people won't believe the Bible, they wouldn't believe if someone rose from the dead. And that is true. A few days later the Lord Jesus raised another man named Lazarus from the dead, and men tried to kill him (John 11:1-53). Later, the Lord rose from the dead Himself, and still men and women don't believe.

"Heavy, man, heavy!" That's what some people say when they come to the subject of hell in the Bible. Many say that there are no such places as Hades and hell. They think it is inconsistent for a God of love to permit such a place as hell to exist. They say that if hell is anywhere, it is here. But what does the Bible say? What did Jesus say?

Hades is a reality and so is hell. The Lord Jesus spoke more about these two places than anyone else. And from what He said about them, they must be very bad.

The Bible teaches that God did not create hell for man. He made it for the devil and his angels (Matthew 25:41). He does not want any human being to go to hell (2 Peter 3:9). He has provided a way of salvation so that no one has to go there. If someone goes to hell, it is because he has refused the only alternative, that is, heaven.

It certainly is clear from the story of the rich man and Lazarus that the spirit and soul do not die when the body dies. In death, the body is said to sleep, but the spirit and soul do not sleep. When a believer dies, his spirit and soul go to be with Christ in heaven (Philippians 1:23; 2 Corinthians 5:6-8). When an unbeliever dies, his spirit and soul go to Hades (Luke

16:19-28). As we have said, Hades is a place of conscious suffering. The rich man in Hades had feeling (v. 23), sight (v. 23), recognition (of Abraham and Lazarus) (v. 23), speech (v. 24), thirst (v. 24), memory (v. 25), hearing (v. 25), and intelligence and reasoning powers (vv. 27-28). The suffering in Hades is a terrible scene (vv. 23-24, 28).

What Really Counts at the End

We also learn from this story that the rich man's wealth couldn't save him from dying. When his time came, he had to go. But we must be clear that he didn't go to Hades because he was rich. Neither did Lazarus go to heaven because he was poor. The thing that determines where a man goes at the time of death is whether he has ever believed and received the Lord Jesus Christ as Savior (John 1:12 and 3:16, 36).

It is rather solemn to notice that people in Hades have more of an interest in the salvation of their loved ones than they ever did when they were alive. The rich man wanted someone to go warn his brothers. Someone has said, "There are no unbelievers in hell." They believe—but it is too late.

The great gulf between heaven and Hades (verse 26) reminds us that once a person dies, his eternal destiny is settled. There is no second chance. "Where the tree falls, there it will lie" (Ecclesiastes 11:3). Hades and hell are prisons from which there is no escape.

Abraham told the rich man that his five brothers had the Bible, and that God would not send someone from the dead to them. God holds men and women responsible for reading, believing, and obeying the Bible. He wants us to believe it because it is His Word, the Word of One who cannot lie. If we do not believe it, we are calling Him a liar. God is not pleased by that. Neither is He pleased by the kind of "faith" (really, unbelief) that demands a miracle. Jesus once said to Thomas, "Have you believed because you have seen me? Blessed are those who have not seen and yet have believed" (John 20:29).

To go to Hades, there is nothing a man needs to do. To get out of Hades, there is nothing he *can* do. Those who reject the Savior choose to go to Hades. But so do those who neglect the gospel. Those who say they can't decide have already decided.

Each of us should ask himself, "Where will I go when I die? Where will I spend eternity?" Those who repent and receive the sinner's Savior can be certain of eternity in heaven with the Lord Jesus Christ.

CHAPTER 5 EXAM

Use the exam answer sheet at the back of the book to complete your exam.

1. **The rich man in Hades**
   A. was unconscious, as though sleeping.
   B. couldn't see or recognize anyone else.
   C. was in terrible suffering.

2. **The rich man went to Hades because**
   A. God was evening up the score of his rich and self-centered life while on earth.
   B. he had despised poor Lazarus.
   C. he had not been a believer in his life on earth.

3. **When we die, the part of us that "sleeps" is**
   A. our spirit.
   B. our soul.
   C. our body.

4. **When you die**
   A. your eternal destiny cannot be changed.
   B. you get a second chance.
   C. you are reincarnated according to how well you lived your life.

5. **Abraham told the rich man that his brothers could learn how to be saved from eternal damnation by**
   A. reading and obeying the holy Scriptures.
   B. seeing a miracle.
   C. feeding poor beggars.

6. **Matthew 25:41 tells us that**
   A. God created hell to punish wicked people.
   B. God made hell for the devil and his angels.
   C. God would never send any creature to hell.

7. Every one of us should read and obey the Bible because

A. it is the best-selling book ever.

B. it is considered good literature.

C. in it we learn how to be saved from eternal judgment.

8. If you reject Christ, you

A. have merely exercised a personal preference in religious matters.

B. will get a second chance after death.

C. have automatically chosen Hades and hell.

9. To be sent to Hades, a person must

A. commit some big sin like murder.

B. deliberately curse God.

C. just leave God out of his or her life.

10. If you repent and receive Christ as Savior, you

A. have a good chance of getting saved.

B. may well make it at last if you hang in there.

C. can be positively certain of an eternity in heaven with Him.

What Do You Say?

Where do you expect to spend eternity? Why?

____

____

____

____

CHAPTER

6

THE LITTLE MAN WHO WAS UP A TREE

He entered Jericho and was passing through. And behold, there was a man named Zacchaeus. He was a chief tax collector and was rich. And he was seeking to see who Jesus was, but on account of the crowd he could not, because he was small in stature. So he ran on ahead and climbed up into a sycamore tree to see him, for he was about to pass that way. And when Jesus came to the place, he looked up and said to him, "Zacchaeus, hurry and come down, for I must stay at your house today." So he hurried and came down and received him joyfully. And when they saw it, they all grumbled, "He has gone in to be the guest of a man who is a sinner." And Zacchaeus stood and said to the Lord, "Behold, Lord, the half of my goods I give to the poor. And if I have defrauded anyone of anything, I restore it fourfold." And Jesus said to him, "Today salvation has come to this house, since he also is a son of Abraham. For the Son of Man came to seek and to save the lost."

–Luke 19:1-10

When the news got around that Jesus was passing through the city of Jericho, crowds lined the main street to get a look at Him. Somewhere in the back of the crowd was a fellow named Zacchaeus (pronounced Zack-ée-us). He was in charge of the local tax office, he was rich, he was of the Jewish religion, and he was too short to see over the heads of the crowd. The fact that he was a tax collector didn't set well with his fellow Jews. What loyal Jew would work for the oppressive Romans? There might be a connection between his work and his riches; tax collectors had earned a reputation for being crooks who took too much money. In spite of all that, he was a big shot in the community and proud of his position.

Now he was very eager to see Jesus. Undoubtedly he had heard about this Jewish Preacher who performed miracles and whose teachings had the ring of truth about them. Certainly he had heard that the religious leaders were almost solidly against Jesus while many of the common people were just as enthusiastically for Him. Zacchaeus had more than an idle curiosity. He had a growing conviction that this Jesus offered something he needed—a new life. So he wanted to see Jesus for himself.

The Son of Man came to seek and to save the lost.

The only trouble was that he was too short. It seems as if there are always obstacles when men and women want to see Jesus. This time, it was the crowd that was in the way. Can't you picture him bobbing back and forth at the rear, looking for an opening? But there was no opening.

Then he had an idea. He could climb that tree over there. But wait. What would people think? After all, he was the local director of Internal Revenue. It would hardly do for the chief tax collector to climb a tree!

Forgetting Your Image

But there was no time to think of his importance. He could tell by the rising chatter of the crowd that Jesus was getting near. It was his hour of decision. He climbed up the tree and sat on the first branch—a ringside seat. When Zacchaeus saw Jesus, something happened inside him. He knew at that minute that he needed to make a choice—he needed to follow Him. In his heart, he became a disciple of the Master. It was a definite act of faith.

That act of faith didn't escape Jesus as He was God, and therefore knew of Zacchaeus's change of heart. As He passed the tree, He looked up, and saw Zacchaeus and called out to him, "Come down quickly. I'd like to stay at your house today."

Zacchaeus jumped down from the tree, ran through the crowd to meet Jesus, and proudly escorted Him to his house. It was the greatest honor he had ever had.

Some of his neighbors, especially the "clergy," were green with envy and ticked off that Jesus would pass by the homes of decent, respectable people only to stay with a detested tax collector.

Inside the house, Zacchaeus was thinking of all the money he had taken illegally. Now that he was a follower of Jesus, he realized that he should pay back what he had stolen. So he turned to the Lord Jesus and promised two things: first, that he would give half of his money to the poor, and second, that he would repay $4.00 for every dollar he had stolen. Actually, the law didn't require him to do this. All he had to do was give a tenth of his income and repay $1.20 for each dollar he had taken illegally. But he was being guided now by a higher principle than that of the law.

Jesus realized, of course, that Zacchaeus was now a true believer. He said "Today salvation has come to this house, since he also is a son of Abraham." Meaning, you have demonstrated the same kind of faith as your ancestor, Abraham. And then, as if to answer those outside who were criticizing him for going to a sinner's house, Jesus said, "The Son of Man came to seek and to save the lost."

Getting Around the Obstacles

Now if we take a second look at this story, we find several valuable lessons lying beneath the surface.

Zacchaeus was rich, but he felt the need for something more than gold. It is possible to be rich as far as the world is concerned and yet to be poor as far as God is concerned. On the other hand, a man may be poor in goods and yet be rich spiritually. If he is a believer, he is an heir of God and a joint heir with Jesus Christ.

This rich man found that when he wanted to see Jesus, there were problems. The crowd, for instance, was an obstacle. Sometimes it's pride that is in the way. Sometimes it's the fear of man (see Proverbs 29:25). Sometimes it's riches. And sometimes it's the unwillingness to give up some favorite sin.

But whatever the obstacle might be, true faith does not allow it to prevent the person from coming to Jesus. Where there is a desire to follow the Lord, there will always be a way. Doubt sees the obstacles; faith finds a way.

Faith never goes unnoticed by the Savior.

And faith never goes unnoticed by the Savior. Whenever a man repents of his sins and receives Jesus Christ as Lord and Savior, the Lord knows about it and writes that man's name in His book of life. The man doesn't have to say a word out loud. He doesn't have to raise his hand or go forward in a church service. All he has to do is receive the Lord Jesus as his Savior from sin. Of course, after he does this, he will want to tell others about the Lord. He won't want to keep it a secret.

If on Jesus Christ you trust,
Speak for Him you surely must,
Though it humble to the dust;
If you love Him, say so.

The Smartest Thing He Ever Did

Climbing that tree was the best thing Zacchaeus ever did. That act of faith brought blessings to him that he never dreamed of. For instance, he was privileged to have the Son of God as a guest in his house that day. Then too, the story of how he met Jesus has become a part of the Bible, so that Zacchaeus is known to us in the 21st century. Finally, Zacchaeus was assured of salvation and of a home in heaven forever. When a man trusts Christ, he never knows at the time all the wonderful things that will result from that decision.

One of the most important lessons we learn from this true story is that when a man becomes a Christian, he should try to make right the wrong things he has done, whenever possible. If he has stolen tools, he should return them. If he has taken money, he should give it back. If he has wronged people, he should go to them and make it right. This, incidentally, provides a wonderful opportunity of witnessing for Christ. He can say something like this: "When I was working for you seven years ago, I stole these tools from you. But now I'm a Christian. I was saved last month, and the Lord has been showing me that I should return them to you. Please forgive me for having taken them." Of course, we realize that it is not always possible to make things right. You may no longer have the address of the person, or he may have died. But whenever it is possible, making things right is the Christian thing to do.

When a man becomes a Christian, he should try to make right the wrong things he has done, whenever possible.

There is no question that Zacchaeus had been a sinner; he admitted it. But just because a man has sinned or has failed doesn't mean that God is through with him. Christ's purpose in coming into the world was to seek and to save the lost—not "good" people, but the lost. Actually all people are lost by nature, but most are not willing to admit it. And this unwillingness shuts them off from salvation. Only people who know and admit they are lost can be saved.

This was Christ's last visit to Jericho. He was on His way to Jerusalem to die on the cross. So, in a sense, it was Zacchaeus's last chance to see the Savior. Suppose he had missed his chance! Actually, we never know when it is *our* last chance. We never know when we are hearing the gospel invitation for the last time. That's why it's dangerous to delay. That's why the Bible says, "Behold, now is the accepted time; behold, now is the day of salvation" (2 Corinthians 6:2 KJV).

CHAPTER 6 EXAM

Use the exam answer sheet at the back of the book to complete your exam.

1. Zacchaeus climbed the tree because

A. he was being crushed in the crowd.
B. he wanted to see Jesus.
C. he wanted to get away from Jesus.

2. Jesus knew Zacchaeus had become His disciple because

A. Zacchaeus told him so.
B. Zacchaeus raised his hand in church.
C. Jesus was God and knew of his change of heart.

3. The fact that Zacchaeus was a sinner was

A. not known by his neighbors.
B. not known by the Lord Jesus.
C. known by everyone.

4. Which statement is correct?

A. A rich man has it made for both time and eternity.
B. The poor man is a loser in this life and in eternity.
C. A man's poverty or wealth has nothing to do with salvation, for all men are lost and need a Savior.

5. When we become Christians, we should

A. try to make right the wrong things we have done.
B. just forget the wrongs we have done to others.
C. hope others forgive us just as God does.

6. Climbing that tree was the smartest thing Zacchaeus ever did because

A. he could see everyone else.
B. it made him feel important.
C. he got saved and Jesus told him so.

7. **Those who are lost and need a Savior are**
   A. only immoral people.
   B. only people with no religious faith.
   C. all moral, immoral, religious, and non-religious people.

8. **Once a person becomes a Christian it is important that he "makes things right." This means**
   A. repaying or making good for past wrongs, especially in dishonest dealings.
   B. forgetting what he has done.
   C. adding good works to his belief in Christ.

9. **When we make good our past mistakes to someone, it is**
   A. a good way to impress people.
   B. most likely to be rejected.
   C. a good opportunity to witness to the change that Christ has effected.

10. **Salvation came to Zacchaeus that day because**
   A. he was a loyal descendant of the Jewish nation.
   B. he decided to go straight.
   C. he put his trust in the Lord Jesus.

What Do You Say?

In what way was Zacchaeus better off when he became a believer in Christ and gave away so much of his money?

____

____

____

____

CHAPTER

7

THE WOMAN WHO WAS CAUGHT IN THE ACT

Early in the morning he came again to the temple. All the people came to him, and he sat down and taught them. The scribes and the Pharisees brought a woman who had been caught in adultery, and placing her in the midst they said to him, "Teacher, this woman has been caught in the act of adultery. Now in the Law Moses commanded us to stone such women. So what do you say?" This they said to test him, that they might have some charge to bring against him. Jesus bent down and wrote with his finger on the ground. And as they continued to ask him, he stood up and said to them, "Let him who is without sin among you be the first to throw a stone at her." And once more he bent down and wrote on the ground. But when they heard it, they went away one by one, beginning with the older ones, and Jesus was left alone with the woman standing before him. Jesus stood up and said to her, "Woman, where are they? Has no one condemned you?" She said, "No one, Lord." And Jesus said, "Neither do I condemn you; go, and from now on sin no more."

–John 8:2-11

Early one morning, Jesus came to the temple area in Jerusalem and, as He often did, began to teach the people who gathered around Him.

The religious leaders didn't like to see the crowds showing an interest in Jesus and in His teachings, so they decided to make Him look bad in the eyes of the people.

They dragged a woman in front of Him and announced rather smugly that they had caught her in the very act of adultery. They reminded Jesus that, according to the law of God, she should be stoned to death (Leviticus 20:10; Deuteronomy 22:22). Then they asked Him for His verdict.

What they were really trying to do was trap the Lord. If He said to stone her, then He was not gracious. If He said to free her, then He was not upholding the law. Either way, He would be wrong.

Before answering them, Jesus stooped down and wrote something in the dust on the ground. All kinds of guesses have been made as to what He wrote, but they are only guesses. The plain fact is that no one knows what He wrote.

The accusers pressed Him harder to get an answer from Him. They kept peppering Him with questions as to what should be done with this guilty woman.

It was then that the Lord Jesus straightened Himself up to His full height and said, "Let him who is without sin among you [or without the same sin] be the first to throw a stone at her."

Again, He stooped down and wrote on the ground. And again, the mystery as to the words remains. No one knows what the message was, and it is useless to try to guess.

But the words of Jesus convicted the scribes and Pharisees. Their trap had backfired on them. In their hearts, were they any different from her? They began to slink away, one by one, from the oldest to the youngest.

Then Jesus said to the woman about her accusers, "Where where are they? Has no one condemned you?" She answered, "No one, Lord." To which Jesus responded, "Neither do I condemn you; go and from now on sin no more."

Is Sin Okay with God?

It would be easy for someone reading this incident carelessly to assume that Jesus actually excused the woman's adultery. But that is not the case, as we shall see. Let us take a second look at the story and see what lessons we can learn from it.

First of all, we see the sex discrimination practiced by the scribes and Pharisees. They cruelly exposed the *woman* who was caught in act of adultery, but what about the *man*? It takes two to commit adultery. They shielded the man and put all the blame and shame on the woman. That is not unusual. The tendency of human kind and human law has often been to punish the woman and let the man go free.

The penalty for committing adultery, under the law of God, was death by stoning. Notice carefully that Jesus did not disregard the law. He did not say that in this case they should forget the law. No, He actually supported the law and instructed them to carry out the sentence. "Let him who is without sin among you be the first to throw a stone at her." This is very important. It would not have been righteous for Jesus to disregard the law or act as if it didn't matter. He must uphold the law.

It is possible that what Jesus actually said or meant was, "Let him who is without *that* sin (the sin of adultery) throw the first stone." If a man was guilty of the same sin, he, too, should be stoned. The sentence should be executed only by someone who was not guilty of the same sin. The fact that all the scribes and Pharisees left shows that they all had a guilty conscience.

Jesus was full of grace and truth.

Notice that in verse 11 the woman addressed Jesus as Lord. We may assume that this was a confession of faith in Him. If this is true, then she was saying, in effect: "I know that I am a guilty sinner. I was caught in the act. But I believe Jesus is the promised Messiah. I yield myself to His authority."

The reply that Jesus made convinces us that she truly repented and believed on Him. He said, "Neither do I condemn you; go, and from now on sin no more." This answer shows that Jesus was full of grace and truth (John 1:17). "Neither do I condemn you"—that is grace. "Go and from now on sin no more"—that is truth. The speech of the Lord Jesus was always with grace, seasoned with salt (Colossians 4:6). The first part here was grace; the second was salt.

"Neither do I condemn you." That is what the Savior says to everyone who seeks forgiveness and pardon from Him. There is no condemnation to those who are in Christ Jesus (Romans 8:1). He promised that those who hear His word and believe on the One who sent Him would never enter into condemnation (John 5:24). See also John 3:17-19.

Then Jesus added, "Go and from now on sin no more." But why did He say this? Didn't He know that even those who are true believers still sin every day in thought, word, and deed? Yes, He knew all that. But He wanted to set before this woman His perfect standard. His will is that we should not sin at all (1 John 2:1). God cannot accept sin as right. If Jesus had said, "Go and sin just a little," we would know He was not God, because God is holy and cannot approve any sin (Habakkuk 1:13). So the Lord gave her His ideal for the Christian life—"Go and from now on sin no more."

What Happens When You Don't Live Right?

Someone will ask, "What happens if a Christian does sin?" In considering this subject, there are several things that should be noted.

1. A Christian is not sinless, but he does sin less (Romans 6:14).
2. When a Christian sins, he does not lose his salvation, but he does lose the joy of his salvation (Psalm 51:12). His relationship with God is not broken; he is still a son. But his fellowship with God is broken; the happy family spirit is gone.
3. The penalty of all the sins of a believer was paid by the Lord Jesus at the cross of Calvary (Isaiah 53:6). When Jesus died, all our sins were future, and He died for them all. Because Jesus paid the debt, I will not have to. God does not demand payment twice. There is no double jeopardy.
4. This does not mean that a Christian can sin and get away with it. The believer has his security, but God still has His "woodshed." Even though the penalty has been paid, which means that I will never have to go to hell, it is still true that sin has its effects in this life. The believer who sins may expect the discipline of God. It may be in the form of sickness, of some sorrow, of some loss, or accident, or even death itself (see 1 Corinthians 11:27-32).

   A Christian is not sinless, but he does sin less

5. Any unconfessed sin in the believer's life will result in loss of reward at the judgment seat of Christ (1 Corinthians 3:12-15). Time spent out of fellowship with God is time wasted for all eternity.
6. God has made provision for a believer when he sins. We read in 1 John 2:1—"If anyone does sin, we have an advocate with the Father, Jesus Christ the righteous." He pleads the believer's cause before God the Father and says, "Charge that to My account." He represents the sinning believer and works tirelessly to bring that person to the place where he will confess and forsake his sin (Proverbs 28:13).
7. The moment a believer confesses his sin, he is forgiven, and the happy family spirit is restored. "If we confess our sins, he is faithful and just to forgive us our sins and to cleanse us from all unrighteousness." (1 John 1:9).

8. When a person is saved, the Holy Spirit of God comes to dwell inside him (1 Corinthians 6:19). The Holy Spirit gives him the power to resist temptation. The believer cannot say, "I had to sin," or "The devil made me do it." The Holy Spirit will give him the power to say NO. If he calls on the Lord in the moment of fierce temptation, the Lord will give him victory over sin. "The name of the LORD is a strong tower; the righteous man runs into it and is safe" (Proverbs 18:10).

There is a curious twist to the story of the woman caught in the act. The accused woman will be in heaven, while her accusers will be in hell (if they didn't repent later). That is why Jesus said to the religious leaders on one occasion, "I say to you, the tax collectors and the prostitutes go into the kingdom of God before you" (Matthew 21:31). She probably thought she was a born loser. As it turned out, she was born to win.

CHAPTER 7 EXAM

Use the exam answer sheet at the back of the book to complete your exam.

1. **In the incident conveyed in Chapter 7 the religious leaders were trying to**
   A. raise the moral standards of their community.
   B. trap the Lord Jesus and get Him into trouble.
   C. show the people how good they were in comparison.

2. **Why did Jesus say, "He who is without sin among you, let him throw a stone at her first"?**
   A. So that the people could see who was the most righteous
   B. Because He was trying to get around the law
   C. So that each man would begin to think and realize that he was guilty of sinning as well as the accused woman

3. **When the woman addressed Jesus as "Lord," she was saying in effect,**
   A. I believe that Jesus is a good man.
   B. I believe that Jesus is the promised Messiah.
   C. I believe that Jesus is royalty.

4. **"Neither do I condemn you" illustrates Jesus'**
   A. grace.
   B. truth.
   C. compromising attitude.

5. **Jesus' command to "Go and sin no more"**
   A. sets a perfect standard.
   B. is not to be taken literally.
   C. illustrates the fanaticism of early Christian ideas.

6. **When we become Christians,**
   A. only our past sins are forgiven.
   B. the penalty for all our sins (past and future) has been paid.
   C. we dare not sin at all or we'll be lost again.

7. **When a Christian sins,**
   A. he loses his salvation.
   B. he loses his relationship with God entirely.
   C. his fellowship with God is broken.

8. **Because the penalty of the believer's sin has been paid at the cross,**
   A. Christians can sin with no consequences.
   B. Christians can still expect to be disciplined (the "woodshed") for sin through bad health, problems, or even death.
   C. punishment here and now must be atoned for by man through penance and offerings to the church.

9. **If a believer confesses his sin,**
   A. God will immediately forgive it.
   B. he should also fast to expect fully forgiveness.
   C. he may hope for forgiveness if he is properly absolved by a minister or priest.

10. **When the accused woman was brought to the Lord Jesus, she**
   A. gained everything worthwhile in getting to know Him.
   B. lost her reputation forever.
   C. refused to admit her guilt.

EXAM 7

What Do You Say?

What do you think God thinks about you? Would He find you guilty as you stand right now? Can you genuinely call Him "Lord"?

CHAPTER

8

THE GREATEST CRIME EVER COMMITTED

There was also an inscription over him, "This is the King of the Jews." One of the criminals who were hanged railed at him, saying, "Are you not the Christ? Save yourself and us!" But the other rebuked him, saying, "Do you not fear God, since you are under the same sentence of condemnation? And we indeed justly, for we are receiving the due reward of our deeds; but this man has done nothing wrong." And he said, "Jesus, remember me when you come into your kingdom." And he said to him, "Truly, I say to you, today you will be with me in Paradise."

It was now about the sixth hour, and there was darkness over the whole land until the ninth hour, while the sun's light failed. And the curtain of the temple was torn in two. Then Jesus, calling out with a loud voice, said, "Father, into your hands I commit my spirit!" And having said this he breathed his last. Now when the centurion saw what had taken place, he praised God, saying, "Certainly this man was innocent!" And all the crowds that had assembled for this spectacle, when they saw what had taken place, returned home beating their breasts. And all his acquaintances and the women who had followed him from Galilee stood at a distance watching these things.

Now there was a man named Joseph, from the Jewish town of Arimathea. He was a member of the council, a good and righteous man, who had not consented to their decision and action; and he was looking for the kingdom of God. This man went to Pilate and asked for the body of Jesus. Then he took it down and wrapped it in a linen shroud and laid him in a tomb cut in stone, where no one had ever yet been laid. It was the day of Preparation, and the Sabbath was beginning. The women who had come with him from Galilee followed and saw the tomb and how his body was laid. Then they returned and prepared spices and ointments. On the Sabbath they rested according to the commandment.

–Luke 23:38-56 (see also Matthew 27:37-66; Mark 15:26-47; John 19:19-42)

The scene of the crime was outside the walls of the city of Jerusalem. It was the place where the death penalty was usually carried out. The Jews called it Golgotha. The Romans called it Calvary. Today, we would probably call it Skull Hill. It was alongside one of the main roads leading to the city.

On a Friday morning, years ago, some Roman soldiers brought a Man there to be executed. He was in His early thirties. He and the soldiers were followed by an angry, shouting mob—people whose mouths and jaws were twisted into expressions of murderous hate. They yelled, they jeered, they cursed, they hurled insults, they mocked. No question that they were out for blood—His blood.

And who was this supposed Criminal? His Name was Jesus. He was born in Bethlehem, and grew up in Nazareth. He had followed His stepfather and become a carpenter. But then when He was about thirty, He left His tools and started off on what you might call a crusade, with real fire and dedication. That's when the trouble started. The things He taught and the claims He made for Himself put Him on a direct collision course with the religious leaders. They made several unsuccessful attempts to kill Him. Finally, with the treasonable help of Judas, one of Jesus' own disciples, they had Him captured and arrested. After an illegal court judgment, they turned Him over to the Romans (because the Jews didn't have the authority to carry out capital punishment). The Roman governor found Him "not guilty," but then he folded under pressure from the religious leaders and turned Him over to the execution squad. That gives you a brief sketch of the life of Jesus.

Who Was the Man? Why Did He Die?

But there's more that you must know. Jesus was not just a man. He was much, much more. He was the Son of God. He was the great God of the universe, visiting our planet in a human body. He was the One who created everything, and He's the One who holds everything together (John 1:10; Colossians 1:17).

Our all-powerful Creator had to become a mortal human being so that He could *die* (since God, being eternal, cannot die). He came to die as our substitute, to pay the penalty for our sins that we should have paid. He came to provide a way by which we can spend eternity with Him in heaven.

But who was really to blame for the death of Jesus? Well, the religious leaders and all the people were certainly to blame; they said, "His blood be on us and on our children" (Matthew 27:25). The Roman authorities were also to blame because they were the ones who actually executed Him. But we don't see the whole picture unless we realize that we are *all* guilty of His death because it was our sins that nailed Him to the cross. He died for the sins of the whole world (1 Peter 3:18; 1 John 2:2).

Jesus came to provide a way by which we can spend eternity with Him in heaven.

As for the actual crucifixion, it happened this way. Soon after they arrived at Calvary, the soldiers offered Jesus a drink of vinegar and gall. This was given to condemned prisoners to help them stand the pain. Jesus would not drink it. He had work to do, and He was not going to do it in a half-drugged condition.

At 9 a.m., they nailed Him to the cross, hands and feet, then lifted up the cross and dropped it into its socket in the ground. It blows your mind—that the Creator should be crucified by the creatures His own hands had made! Yet that's what happened. It was the greatest crime ever committed.

The Maker of the universe
As man—for man—was made a curse . . .
His holy fingers made the boughs
That grew the thorns that crowned His brow.
The nails that pierced His hands were mined
In secret places He designed.
He made the forest where there sprung
The tree on which His body hung.
He died upon a cross of wood,
Yet made the hill on which it stood.

It was a custom for the soldiers to divide the clothes of condemned men among themselves. They did this with the clothes of Jesus—except His seamless robe. They gambled for that. This fulfilled a prophecy which David made centuries earlier, "They divide my garments among them, and for my clothing they cast lots" (Psalm 22:18).

Over the head of Jesus, they put a sign which was supposed to state His crime. It said simply, "Jesus of Nazareth, the King of the Jews" (John 19:19). Many people didn't like that. They wanted Pilate, the governor, to change it to read, "This man said, I am the King of the Jews." But Pilate wouldn't budge.

When people die, their relatives and friends are often interested to know what were the last words they spoke. Jesus said seven important things as He hung on the cross. The first was, "Father, forgive them, for they know not what they do" (Luke 23:34). This was a terrific show of grace—that He should pray for His guilty murderers. The prayer means that even they could have been saved if they had repented and believed in Him.

Taking the Rap for Others

The angry mob was not in a mood to repent but was whipping itself up into a hysterical frenzy. The people who happened to be passing by said, "You who would destroy the temple and rebuild it in three days, save yourself! If you are the Son of God, come down from the cross" (Matthew 27:40). The religious leaders mocked Jesus, yelling, "He saved others; he cannot save himself. He is the King of Israel; let him come down now from the cross, and we will believe in him. He trusts in God; let God deliver him now, if he desires him. For he said, 'I am the Son of God'" (Matthew 27:42-43). The true fact, of course, is that if Jesus had saved Himself, then you and I could never have been saved. He could have come down from the cross, but that would have defeated His purpose in coming into the world, which was to give His life as a ransom for us.

Then from the cross there came the Savior's promise to the dying thief, "Today you will be with me in Paradise." We'll take a look at his story in the next chapter.

Mary, the broken hearted mother of Jesus, was standing in the crowd. As Jesus looked down upon her with compassion, He told the apostle John to take care of her. He had no pity for Himself, but oceans of pity for others.

The Lord Jesus suffered the punishment that we deserved.

From noon till 3 p.m., thick darkness covered the whole scene. It seemed that nature was showing sympathy for what was happening on the middle cross. As an old hymn put it:

Well might the sun in darkness hide
And shut His glories in,
When Christ, the mighty Maker, died
For man, His creature's sin.

It was during those three hours that the Lord Jesus bore the awful anger of God against our sins. He suffered the punishment that we deserved. He endured the concentrated horrors of hell that should have been ours for all eternity. No one will ever know what He went through. The physical sufferings were bad enough, but they were nothing compared to the spiritual suffering of being utterly forsaken by God. And it was all for you and for me!

What It Took to Finish the Job

At the close of the three hours of darkness, Jesus cried loudly, "My God, my God, why have you forsaken me?" (Matthew 27:46) We know the answer. Our sins had been put on Jesus. God's holiness and righteousness demanded that those sins be punished. When God saw our sins on His own beloved Son, He forsook Him. And so Jesus paid the penalty of those sins for us. He was forsaken so that we might never be forsaken.

Then Jesus cried, "I thirst." We can think of that in two ways. First of all, He suffered intense physical thirst after hanging on the cross for at least six hours. But it may be that He was also expressing His spiritual thirst for the salvation of men and women. Thinking that Jesus meant physical thirst, one of the soldiers attached a sponge full of vinegar to a pole and lifted it to Jesus' lips.

As soon as He had swallowed some of the vinegar, Jesus exclaimed, "It is finished!" He had finished the work which God had sent Him to do. He had provided a way by which God could save guilty sinners. He had fully satisfied all the claims of God against our sins. And because He finished the work, we can't add to it, and we don't need to. All we have to do is trust the One who finished the work.

At last, the Savior cried, "Father, into your hands I commit my spirit." And as soon as He said this, He yielded up His life, that is, He died. The important point to notice here is that He controlled the time of His death. We can't do that. We die when the time comes. But Christ had power to lay down His life (John 10:18).

One of the Roman officers must have sensed that something very unusual was taking place, because he commented, "Certainly this was innocent!" "Truly this man was the Son of God!" (Luke 23:47; Mark 15:39).

At the very time Jesus died, two strange things happened. The heavy curtain that separated the two rooms of the temple in Jerusalem was torn from the top to the bottom (a divine object-lesson that the way into God's presence was now open). Also, there was an earthquake, which split open many graves (perhaps an indication that Christ had broken the power of death).

As was customary, the soldiers broke the legs of the two thieves on the other two crosses to hasten death, but when they came to Jesus and saw that He had already died, they didn't break His legs. But one of them pierced His side with a spear, causing blood and water to flow out.

A secret follower of Jesus, Joseph of Arimathea, took the body down from the cross and placed it in a tomb he had carved out of rock.

But that is not the end of the story. Three days later, Jesus rose from the dead! And forty days after that, He went back to heaven where He sits today at God's right hand, a Prince and a Savior.

It is a fact of history that Jesus rose from the dead. That is how we know that Christianity is the only true religion. All other founders of religion are dead and their bodies are in graves. But Christ is alive in heaven. Only a fool would trust his soul to a dead person. But a wise man trusts his soul to a living Savior, the Lord Jesus Christ.

A wise man trusts his soul to a living Savior, the Lord Jesus Christ.

The greatest crime ever committed was when men crucified the Lord of life and glory. But God overruled it for our eternal blessing—if we will only believe that Christ died as our Substitute and receive Him into our life.

CHAPTER 8 EXAM

Use the exam answer sheet at the back of the book to complete your exam.

1. **According to the text, who was to blame for Jesus' death?**
   A. The religious leaders who opposed Him
   B. The soldiers who crucified Him
   C. All of us, because it was for all our sins He died

2. **The crucifixion of the Lord Jesus was the greatest crime ever committed because**
   A. He was such a good man.
   B. He was betrayed by one of His own disciples.
   C. He was the Son of God and men hated and rejected Him.

3. **The Son of God came to earth**
   A. to set a heroic example.
   B. to start a new denomination.
   C. to die for us and save us from our sins.

4. **The first thing Jesus said from the cross was**
   A. "I thirst."
   B. "Father, forgive them . . ."
   C. "My God, why have You forsaken Me?"

5. **Thick darkness covered the earth from**
   A. 9 a.m. to 3 p.m.
   B. noon to 3 p.m.
   C. 6 a.m. to noon.

6. **In those hours on the cross, the Lord Jesus bore**
   A. His own punishment for stirring up the crowds against Rome.
   B. the sins of the Jewish nation only.
   C. the punishment we all deserve.

7. **Why did God forsake Jesus on the cross?**
   A. Because He is holy and was judging Jesus for our sins in our place
   B. Because Jesus should have avoided being caught and executed
   C. Because God could do nothing to help Him

8. When Jesus cried, "It is finished," He meant that

A. His human life was over .

B. His cause and program had been defeated .

C. He had finished the work God had sent Him to do.

9. In the poem quoted in this chapter, Christ is referred to as

A. the Maker.

B. the Example.

C. the Son.

10. The heavy temple curtain was torn when Jesus died to show that

A. God was angry at the crucifixion of His Son.

B. the way into God's presence was now open.

C. the priests were sorry for putting Jesus to death.

What Do You Say?

What meaning does Jesus' death on the cross have for you? Do you believe He died for you? Have you thanked Him?

____

____

____

____

CHAPTER

9

GETTING LIFE AT THE LAST MINUTE

Two others, who were criminals, were led away to be put to death with him.

–Luke 23:32

One of the criminals who were hanged railed at him, saying, "Are you not the Christ? Save yourself and us!" But the other rebuked him, saying, "Do you not fear God, since you are under the same sentence of condemnation? And we indeed justly, for we are receiving the due reward of our deeds; but this man has done nothing wrong." And he said, "Jesus, remember me when you come into your kingdom." And he said to him, "Truly, I say to you, today you will be with me in Paradise."

–Luke 23:39-43

Jesus was not the only one who was crucified that day. Two bandits were also hung on crosses, one on each side of Him. Seven hundred years earlier, the prophet Isaiah had predicted that the coming Messiah would be "numbered with the transgressors" (or criminals) (see Isaiah 53:12). Now that prophecy had been fulfilled.

At first, the two bandits joined the crowd in taunting Jesus (Mark 15:32). That seems rather strange—that two criminals, in the agonies of crucifixion, could find time to mock the sinless Savior who was hanging next to them. They were saying, in effect, "If You are the One You claim to be—the King of Israel and the Son of God—come down from the cross. Or let God come and rescue You. Save Yourself and us. Then we will believe on You."

But then one of these desperados had a change of heart. He did an about-face—which is another way of saying that he repented. First, he rebuked his fellow-criminal: "Aren't you afraid to talk like that, when you are going to meet God so soon?" he asked. "After all, we are both getting what we deserve, but this Man hasn't done anything wrong."

Then he said to the Lord Jesus, "Lord, remember me when You reign as King." Again, a remarkable thing for one dying man to say to another!

Jesus' answer was great. He said to the penitent thief, "What I tell you is the absolute truth. You are going to be with Me in heaven today."

And so we have the first result of the work of the Lord Jesus on the cross—a dying thief cleansed from his sins and made absolutely fit for heaven.

Now let's, go back over the story and see what we can learn that will help us.

How to Take Sides with God

The first lesson I see is that man is naturally sinful. The two thieves had both been found guilty and sentenced to death, yet in the closing moments of their lives, they still dared to mock and curse the holy Son of God. The Bible is surely right when it says that man is a sinner (see Romans 3:10-18). Deep down inside, man is no good.

Next I see that if a man is going to be saved, he must first change his attitude about his sins. The thief did that. He completely reversed his attitude. He confessed that he was a guilty sinner. He turned away from his sinful life and took sides with God against himself. That is what we must all do. We must acknowledge that we are sinners and that we deserve to be punished by God. God commands all men everywhere to repent (Acts 17:30-31).

But repentance is not enough. We must put our faith in Christ. We must confess Jesus as Lord, that is, as the Master of our lives. The dying thief believed that the One hanging next to him was Lord and he didn't hesitate to confess Him as such. The Bible says that if we confess with our mouth that Jesus is Lord and believe in our heart that God raised Him from the dead, we will be saved (Romans 10:9).

The faith of the repentant thief is seen in his amazing confession, "Jesus, remember me when you come into Your kingdom." He believed, as we have seen, that Jesus is Lord, even over death. He believed that although Jesus was dying at that moment, yet He would rise from the dead. And He believed that Jesus would return some day to reign over the earth. He wanted Jesus to remember him in mercy at that future time. He had great faith in a great Savior.

Another obvious lesson we learn from this incident is that we are not saved by good works. If we were, then this man could never have been saved. His past life had been filled with wicked works. And now it was impossible for him to perform good works because his hands and feet were nailed to the cross. The Bible repeatedly teaches that we are not saved by good deeds (see Ephesians 2:8-9; Titus 3:5). The best we can offer God is nothing but filthy rags in His sight (Isaiah 64:6). When men asked Jesus what good work they should do to please God, He said they should *believe* on the One whom God had sent, that is, the Lord Jesus Himself (John 6:28-29). That is where we must all begin. Then good works will follow salvation. They are the *result* of salvation, not the cause. They are the fruit, not the root. We are not saved *by* good works, but we *are* saved *to perform* good works (Ephesians 2:10).

Good works are the result of salvation, not the cause.

The experience of the dying thief also teaches us that salvation is not by baptism. He was not baptized. It was impossible for him to be baptized. And yet Jesus said that he would be in heaven. Does this mean that we should forget about baptism? No, the Bible teaches that all those who trust the Lord Jesus should make a public confession of Him by being baptized. The thief would probably have been baptized if it had been possible. But the point here is that baptism is not needed for salvation.

Is Salvation a Strange Feeling?

We learn next that it was not by his feelings that he knew he was saved. Many people today have the mistaken idea that when they trust Christ as Savior, they experience some mysterious, happy feelings in their nervous system, and that is how they know they are saved. But if you had asked the thief, "Do you feel saved?" he probably would have replied, "All I feel is pain." How, then, did he know he was saved? He knew because he heard Jesus say, "Today you will be with me in paradise." He knew it because Jesus said so. And that is how believers today know they are saved. The only difference is that today Jesus speaks to us through the Bible, not in an audible voice. In the Bible, Jesus promises that all who believe on Him are saved (see John 5:24). Thus we learn that assurance of salvation comes through the Word of God and not through happy feelings.

Another lesson we learn is that believers go directly to be with Christ in heaven at the time of their death. That is the wonderful truth of Luke 23:43.

Today—the best time.
With Me—the best company.
In Paradise—the best place.

The Christian really has it made. But the passage is a solemn reminder to us that not all are saved. There were two bandits, but only one of them was saved. Someone stated it like this:

One was saved that none may despair.
Only one was saved that none may presume.

From the side of Jesus Christ, one man may go to heaven and another to hell. On which side of the cross are you?

And we also see, of course, that a person can be saved in the last moments of his life. The thief was saved on the very doorstep of eternity. But a person would be foolish to delay getting saved until then, because he never knows which moment will be his last. After all, the Bible says, "Now is the accepted time; behold, now is the day of salvation" (2 Corinthians 6:2 KJV).

One last word! It is frightening how close a person can be to Jesus and still be lost. The other thief was so near and yet so far. So, today, a person can be born and brought up in a Christian family, can be baptized, can join a church, and can engage in Christian activities—yet, if he has never been born again by receiving Christ, he is lost. If he dies in his sins, he will spend eternity in hell.

One of the famous hymns of the Christian faith summarizes the main message of this lesson:

There is a fountain filled with blood,
Drawn from Immanuel's veins;
And sinners plunged beneath that flood
Lose all their guilty stains!
The dying thief rejoiced to see
That fountain in his day;
And there may I, though vile as he,
Wash all my sins away.

CHAPTER 9 EXAM

Use the exam answer sheet at the back of the book to complete your exam.

1. **One of the criminals crucified with Jesus**
   A. was not guilty and was being executed unjustly.
   B. confessed he was a sinner and asked for mercy.
   C. was already one of Jesus' followers.

2. **When a man repents, he**
   A. simply says he is sorry for his sins.
   B. offers to God the good works he has done.
   C. confesses he is a sinner.

3. **The repentant thief**
   A. had great faith in a great Savior.
   B. asked to be taken down from the cross.
   C. believed that death ended everything.

4. **The fact that the dying thief could not be baptized and yet was saved shows that**
   A. baptism is unimportant.
   B. baptism is only for infants.
   C. baptism is not necessary for salvation.

5. **Assurance of salvation comes first and foremost from**
   A. a wonderful feeling inside.
   B. the Word of God.
   C. the authority of the church and its teachers.

6. **Christians are not shocked that their Savior was "numbered with the transgressors" (or criminals) since**
   A. Isaiah had predicted it seven centuries previously.
   B. many criminals are quite nice underneath.
   C. Christians don't shock easily anymore.

7. **The fact that only one of the two bandits got saved**
   A. is a warning that we can be close to Christ and Christian things and still be lost.
   B. shows the unfairness of Christianity.
   C. indicates that half the world will be converted.

8. **We learn from this chapter that**
   A. a person can be saved in the very last moments of life.
   B. it's a good idea to wait to be saved until you're old and about to die.
   C. no one can be sure in this life that he'll go to heaven.

9. **When a Christian dies**
   A. he goes to a place of purification before going to heaven.
   B. he falls asleep and is unconscious of everything.
   C. he goes immediately to be with Christ in heaven.

10. **Second Corinthians 6:2 says that the accepted time to be saved is**
   A. on a Sunday.
   B. during Holy Week.
   C. now.

What Do You Say?

On which side of the cross do you stand? Do you take sides with the repentant man or with the others? Remember, there is no neutral ground—those who do not trust the Savior are on the side of the mob and those who crucified Him.

CHAPTER

10

TWO PREACHERS WHO WENT TO JAIL

As we were going to the place of prayer, we were met by a slave girl who had a spirit of divination and brought her owners much gain by fortune-telling. She followed Paul and us, crying out, "These men are servants of the Most High God, who proclaim to you the way of salvation." And this she kept doing for many days. Paul, having become greatly annoyed, turned and said to the spirit, "I command you in the name of Jesus Christ to come out of her." And it came out that very hour.

But when her owners saw that their hope of gain was gone, they seized Paul and Silas and dragged them into the marketplace before the rulers. And when they had brought them to the magistrates, they said, "These men are Jews, and they are disturbing our city. They advocate customs that are not lawful for us as Romans to accept or practice." The crowd joined in attacking them, and the magistrates tore the garments off them and gave orders to beat them with rods. And when they had inflicted many blows upon them, they threw them into prison, ordering the jailer to keep them safely. Having received this order, he put them into the inner prison and fastened their feet in the stocks.

About midnight Paul and Silas were praying and singing hymns to God, and the prisoners were listening to them, and suddenly there was a great earthquake, so that the foundations of the prison were shaken. And immediately all the doors were opened, and everyone's bonds were unfastened. When the jailer woke and saw that the prison doors were open, he drew his sword and was about to kill himself, supposing that the prisoners had escaped. But Paul cried with a loud voice, "Do not harm yourself, for we are all here." And the jailer called for lights and rushed in, and trembling with fear he fell down before Paul and

Silas. Then he brought them out and said, "Sirs, what must I do to be saved?" And they said, "Believe in the Lord Jesus, and you will be saved, you and your household." And they spoke the word of the Lord to him and to all who were in his house. And he took them the same hour of the night and washed their wounds; and he was baptized at once, he and all his family. Then he brought them up into his house and set food before them. And he rejoiced along with his entire household that he had believed in God.

–Acts 16:16-34

Paul and Silas had gone to Philippi, a city in northern Greece, to preach the gospel. They weren't there long before they became aware of a young demon-possessed woman who earned lots of money for her bosses by telling fortunes. This slave-girl followed Paul and Silas day after day, shouting, "These men are servants of the Most High God, who proclaim to you the way of salvation." She was right. They *were* servants of the Most High God, and they did proclaim *the* way of salvation.

But true or false, Paul would not accept the testimony of a demon. So he finally faced the girl and commanded the demon to come out of her. The slave-girl was instantly delivered. That was good news for her, but it was bad news for her masters, because she had brought them plenty of money. Like so many people, they were more interested in money than in the spiritual welfare of a fellow human being. They decided to get even with the preachers—but how? They would drag them to court and accuse them of anti-Roman activities. The trick worked. The judges were furious. Without a trial, they commanded Paul and Silas to be beaten up and thrown into jail. So that night the two Christian preachers found themselves bruised and bleeding in a maximum security cell, with their feet held fast in stocks.

Did they spend their time feeling sorry for themselves? Forget it. They put their time to good use by praying and singing hymns of praise to God. They knew, as the poet Richard Lovelace said, that "four walls do not a prison make, nor iron bars a cage."

The Duet That Brought Down the House

When Christians pray, you can expect things to happen. At midnight, there was an earthquake that was really a smasher. It opened all the doors and gates of the prison, and even snapped open the stocks that were holding the prisoners' feet. But it didn't flatten the building.

The severe jolt wakened the jailer in his house next door. He bounced out of bed, threw his clothes on and ran outside. What he saw made him surprised and scared! The doors of the prison were wide open. That meant certain death for him, because if any of his prisoners escaped, the only thing for him to do would be to commit suicide. So he drew out his sword and was just about to kill himself when suddenly Paul called out from inside. "Hold it! No need to kill yourself. We're all here."

To believe in Christ is to accept Him as the Way, the Truth, and the Life.

At this moment a tremendous change came over the jailer. Calling for lights, he ran in to the maximum security cell. He was shaking. A moment ago, he was afraid to live; now he was afraid to die. He was not ready to meet God. A tremendous conviction of sin gripped him. His life had been saved, but now he realized that his soul needed to be saved. And so he put the question to Paul and Silas, "What do I have to do to be saved?"

Right away the answer came back, "Believe in the Lord Jesus Christ and you will be saved, and your family can be saved in the same way."

Now let's stop there for a minute! What did Paul and Silas mean by believing in the Lord Jesus Christ?

- Certainly they didn't mean trying to earn or deserve one's salvation. Working is not the same as believing (Romans 4:5).
- They didn't mean trying to keep the Ten Commandments. That's a matter of doing, not believing (Romans 8:3).
- They didn't mean trying to obey the Golden Rule. There's a difference between trying and trusting.
- They didn't mean getting baptized or joining a church. Those things are good, but they should follow believing. Let's not put the cart before the horse.
- They didn't mean just believe the historical facts about Jesus.

What Does It Mean to Believe?

To believe in Christ is to receive Him as Lord and Savior (John 1:12). To believe in Christ is to open the heart's door to him (Revelation 3:20). To believe in Christ is to accept Him as the Way, the Truth, and the Life (John 14:6).

We can believe all the facts about a plane, but we don't really believe it till we get on board and allow it to take us to our destination. Similarly, we must commit ourselves to Jesus as our only hope of heaven.

When I sit on a chair and put all my weight on it, I am trusting the chair. That's what it means to believe on Jesus.

When a woman gets married, she "takes the man to be her lawful, wedded husband." She says, "I do." God says to us, "Do you take My Son to be your Savior from sin?" When we say, "I do," we have believed in the Lord Jesus Christ. When a man can honestly say from the bottom of his heart

1. that he is a sinner and that he deserves to go to hell;
2. that he believes that Jesus died in his place on the cross of Calvary;
3. that he has no other hope for heaven except the Lord Jesus Christ;
4. that he receives the Lord by a definite act of faith;

. . . then that man has believed in Jesus.

That's what the jailer did that night in the jail at Philippi. And the members of his family followed his good example.

Then Paul and Silas gave them some teaching in the Word of the Lord. Among other things, they probably taught that those who believe on the Lord Jesus and are saved should make a public confession of Christ by being baptized.

After this Bible Class, the jailer dressed the wounds of Paul and Silas (you will remember that they had been severely beaten the day before). Then the jailer and his family were baptized, showing that they were now Christians and that they intended to live for the Lord Jesus Christ day by day.

We see that God can bring good out of seemingly bad news.

There was another way in which the jailer showed his new life. He brought the preachers into his house and served them a good meal. If you use a little imagination, you can picture the rejoicing around that table. They were all now one in Christ Jesus, brothers in Christ, and all members of the family of God.

The next day, when the judges learned that Paul and Silas were Roman citizens, they realized that they had made a big mistake in treating these men illegally and brutally. So they made a personal visit to the prison, escorted the prisoners out, and asked them to leave town without any further trouble.

What Was Really Going On?

Now before we leave Paul and Silas, as they move on in their missionary work, there are several points in this incident that we should notice.

First, we notice the different ways in which Satan works. He begins by flattering the two preachers through the lips of the spirit medium. When that didn't work, he resorted to outright persecution, causing Paul and Silas to be beaten and jailed. Sometimes the devil appears as a tricky serpent (Revelation 12:9), and sometimes as a roaring lion (1 Peter 5:8).

Second, in the life of the converted jailer, we see how good works follow salvation. Three good works are mentioned: he dressed the prisoners' wounds; he was baptized; and he took Paul and Silas in and fed them.

As far as Paul and Silas were concerned, we see two men having a tough time for doing good. The Bible tells us that if we are punished for our own wrongdoing, there is no glory for God in that. But if we are punished for well-doing, and bear it patiently, this is pleasing to the Lord (see 1 Peter 2:19-20). After all, that's what happened to Jesus!

We see too that God can bring good (the salvation of the jailer and his household) out of seemingly bad news (the imprisonment of Paul and Silas). God works all things together for good to those who love Him (Romans 8:28).

The timing of the earthquake was perfect. God gives the word to nature to do His work. Those who know God realize that, hidden behind the daily headlines, He is working out His purposes and really winning out.

One final lesson. When the judges had to eat humble pie by personally escorting Paul and Silas out of prison, they demonstrated the truth of Proverbs 16:7: "When a man's ways please the LORD, he makes even his enemies to be at peace with him."

CHAPTER 10 EXAM

Use the exam answer sheet at the back of the book to complete your exam.

1. **The slave-girl who followed Paul**
   A. was sent by God to introduce Paul and his message in Philippi.
   B. was possessed by a demon and being used by Satan.
   C. gave a message that pleased Paul.

2. **Paul and Silas were**
   A. given a fair trial by the Roman officials.
   B. treated kindly when they were thrown into prison.
   C. falsely accused and beaten unjustly.

3. **When Paul and Silas sang and prayed at midnight**
   A. the jailer was angry about the noise.
   B. God was pleased and answered their prayers.
   C. the prisoners were all asleep.

4. **When Christians are busy telling others about the Lord**
   A. Satan doesn't care and leaves them alone.
   B. Satan tries in many ways to stop them.
   C. God doesn't let anyone hurt them.

5. **When things are hard and the news is bad, we know that**
   A. God has given up on us and the world.
   B. Satan is getting the better of God.
   C. God is still in control behind the scenes.

6. **A person who has believed in Jesus**
   A. will always be happy.
   B. believes that Jesus took their punishment on the cross.
   C. experiences deep emotional feelings.

7. **The jailer and his believing family showed their faith in Christ by**
   A. getting baptized.
   B. donating to the church.
   C. reciting the creed.

8. After his conversion, the reality of the jailer's conversion was shown by

A. his belief in all the facts about Jesus.
B. his treating of Paul and Silas' wounds.
C. his carefree happy attitude.

9. This story illustrates that

A. God can bring good out of any bad situation.
B. ancient prisons were poorly built.
C. it doesn't matter what you believe as long as you are sincere.

10. "When a man's ways please the LORD,"

A. "He makes every detail pleasing in His eyes."
B. "He makes even his enemies to be at peace with him."
C. "He will save his soul if he remains faithful to the end."

What Do You Say?

Have you said, "I do," to the Lord Jesus Christ and committed yourself to Him to save you?

CHAPTER

11

THE ADULTERESS WHO BECAME A SOUL WINNER

So he came to a town of Samaria called Sychar, near the field that Jacob had given to his son Joseph. Jacob's well was there; so Jesus, wearied as he was from his journey, was sitting beside the well. It was about the sixth hour.

A woman from Samaria came to draw water. Jesus said to her, "Give me a drink." (For his disciples had gone away into the city to buy food.) The Samaritan woman said to him, "How is it that you, a Jew, ask for a drink from me, a woman of Samaria?" (For Jews have no dealings with Samaritans.) Jesus answered her, "If you knew the gift of God, and who it is that is saying to you, 'Give me a drink,' you would have asked him, and he would have given you living water." The woman said to him, "Sir, you have nothing to draw water with, and the well is deep. Where do you get that living water? Are you greater than our father Jacob? He gave us the well and drank from it himself, as did his sons and his livestock." Jesus said to her, "Everyone who drinks of this water will be thirsty again, but whoever drinks of the water that I will give him will never be thirsty again. The water that I will give him will become in him a spring of water welling up to eternal life." The woman said to him, "Sir, give me this water, so that I will not be thirsty or have to come here to draw water." Jesus said to her, "Go, call your husband, and come here." The woman answered him, "I have no husband." Jesus said to her, "You are right in saying, 'I have no husband'; for you have had five husbands, and the one you now have is not your husband. What you have said is true." The woman said to him, "Sir, I perceive that you are a prophet. Our fathers worshiped on this mountain, but you say that in Jerusalem is the place where people ought to worship." Jesus said to her, "Woman, believe me, the hour is coming when neither on this mountain nor in Jerusalem will you worship the Father. You worship what you do not know; we worship what we know, for salvation is from the Jews. But the hour is coming, and is now here, when the true worshipers will worship the Father in spirit and truth, for the Father is seeking such people to worship him. God is spirit, and those who worship him must worship in spirit and truth." The woman said to him, "I know that Messiah is coming (he who is called Christ). When he comes, he will tell us all things." Jesus said to her, "I who speak to you am he."

Just then his disciples came back. They marveled that he was talking with a woman, but no one said, "What do you seek?" or, "Why are you talking with her?" So the woman left her water jar and went away into town and said to the people, "Come, see a man who told me all that I ever did. Can this be the Christ?" They went out of the town and were coming to him.

–John 4:5-30

Jesus was traveling north from Judea to Galilee. The Jews ordinarily took a roundabout route to avoid going through Samaria; they didn't want to have any contact with the half-breed Samaritans. But Jesus did not believe in racial discrimination, so He took the direct route—right through Samaria.

At noon, weary from His travels, He stopped at a well just as a woman was coming to draw water. He opened the conversation by asking her for a drink. (This surprised her—that a Jew would speak to her, a Samaritan.) That led to a discussion about water in which Jesus spoke of the living water which He offered to people. She kept thinking of the water in the well beside them.

Then Jesus told her that those who drink of this world's "water" will thirst again; nothing that the world can offer will ever satisfy the human heart. But those who drink of the "water" which Jesus gives, that is, the Holy Spirit, will never thirst again.

She was very interested now. She had tried to find satisfaction in sex but had failed. So she asked Him for some of the water He offered so that she would never thirst again.

It was at this point that the Lord Jesus stabbed her conscience with the command, "Go and call your husband." She tried to get off the hook by saying, "I have no husband."

"That's right," said Jesus, "You have no husband. You've had five husbands, and the man you're living with now is not *your* husband."

In saying this Jesus was not trying to shame or embarrass her. He was only trying to show her that she was living in sin. A relationship like hers was contrary to the word of God. In fact, any sex outside of the true marriage relationship is sinful. Some people say today that anything is okay as long as it's done in "love." They say that any sex acts are all right as long as they are done by consenting adults. But the Bible says No! They are sin. (1 Corinthians 6:9-10).

Before this woman could be saved, she had to realize that she was lost. That is why Jesus brought up her sinful past.

Gradually the light dawned on her soul. She came to realize that Jesus was the long-promised Messiah (Christ). She trusted Him as her Lord and Savior, then she went back into the city and boldly confessed Him before others by saying, "Come, see a man who told me all that I ever did. Can this be the Christ?"

Before you can be saved, you must realize that you are lost.

As a result of her witness, many of the Samaritans went out to meet Jesus and became believers in Him. She was not satisfied to keep the blessings of her new-found faith to herself; she wanted to be a channel of blessing to others. And so should we.

To help us in this, we should observe Jesus, the Master Soul Winner, at work. How did He lead the woman away from her sins to saving faith? What was His approach?

First of all, He asked a favor. He broke the ice by requesting a drink of water (John 4:7).

Second, He got her wondering who He was and what was the "living water" which He offered (v. 10). It is important for us to keep people's attention on the Person of Christ and on the salvation which He offers as a free gift.

As she raised questions and difficulties (v. 12), He courteously answered them (vv. 13, 14), but always kept the conversation on target.

When she seemed anxious to receive the living water (v. 15), Jesus awakened her conscience concerning her sinful life (v. 16). People must be brought to acknowledge that they are guilty, lost sinners before they can ever be saved.

She tried to hide the facts concerning her sins, but the Lord showed her that she was living in adultery (vv. 17-18).

Avoiding the Tough Issue

The woman then tried to avoid the issue by talking about differences between the Jewish and Samaritan religions (vv. 20-21)—anything to keep Christ from seeing the fugitive soul in full flight from itself.

Jesus patiently answered by giving her a lesson on the nature of true worship (vv. 22-24).

When she raised the subject of the coming Messiah (Christ), Jesus revealed Himself to her as that very One (vv. 25-26).

It must have been at this point that she surrendered to the Savior, because she went back into the city and invited others to come and meet Him (v. 29). Her witness was simple and effective. The people left their homes and their work and went out to find Jesus.

If we really believe something, we will want to share it with others. She really believed in Christ, and she felt compelled to tell others about Him.

Some believed on the Lord Jesus because of her testimony (v. 39); many more believed because of the words of the Lord Jesus Himself (v. 42).

Think of the miracle that had taken place. In a few short hours, the woman of Samaria had turned away from her sinful life; she had become a worshipping follower of the Messiah of Israel; and she began immediately to invite others to come to Him. That is what God wants to happen in your life.

CHAPTER 11 EXAM

Use the exam answer sheet at the back of the book to complete your exam.

1. **To break the ice in the conversation, Jesus**
   A. discussed the differences between the Jewish and Samaritan faith.
   B. asked for a favor, a drink of water.
   C. brought up the woman's sinful past.

2. **Jesus told the woman that**
   A. this world's "water" satisfies.
   B. nothing the world can offer will ever satisfy the human heart.
   C. the water in Jacob's well wasn't safe to drink.

3. **Jesus said that people should always worship God**
   A. in Jerusalem.
   B. in a synagogue or church.
   C. in spirit and truth.

4. **The Samaritan woman**
   A. had never heard of the Messiah.
   B. met the Messiah Himself in the person of Jesus.
   C. thought the Messiah would be a Samaritan.

5. **According to the Bible, the following is (are) sin:**
   A. fornication, or sex between an unmarried couple.
   B. adultery, or sex where at least one is married.
   C. both of these.

6. **In order to be saved, we, like the Samaritan woman, need to see that we are**
   A. not religious enough.
   B. in the wrong denomination.
   C. lost.

7. **When Jesus revealed that He was the Christ, the woman**
   A. believed Him.
   B. laughed at Him.
   C. argued some more about how to worship God.

8. At the end of the conversation, the woman

A. gave Jesus a drink from the well.
B. invited Jesus to come to her city.
C. went back to the city to tell others about Jesus, the Christ.

9. In witnessing for Christ, it is important to emphasize

A. the Person of Christ and the salvation He freely offers.
B. being in the right religious denomination.
C. straightening out one's life before one can make a commitment.

10. The Samaritan woman wanted to share her knowledge of the Messiah because

A. it was expected of her by the law of Moses.
B. she really believed in Him and wanted others to know Him.
C. Christ commanded her to do it.

What Do You Say?

Have you learned a lesson from the Savior that you want to tell others about?

____

____

____

____

CHAPTER

12

A BUM RAP

Now Joseph had been brought down to Egypt, and Potiphar, an officer of Pharaoh, the captain of the guard, an Egyptian, had bought him from the Ishmaelites who had brought him down there. The LORD was with Joseph, and he became a successful man, and he was in the house of his Egyptian master. His master saw that the LORD was with him and that the LORD caused all that he did to succeed in his hands. So Joseph found favor in his sight and attended him, and he made him overseer of his house and put him in charge of all that he had.

–Genesis 39:1-4

And after a time his master's wife cast her eyes on Joseph and said, "Lie with me." But he refused and said to his master's wife, "Behold, because of me my master has no concern about anything in the house, and he has put everything that he has in my charge. He is not greater in this house than I am, nor has he kept back anything from me except you, because you are his wife. How then can I do this great wickedness and sin against God?" And as she spoke to Joseph day after day, he would not listen to her, to lie beside her or to be with her. But one day, when he went into the house to do his work and none of the men of the house was there in the house, she caught him by his garment, saying, "Lie with me." But he left his garment in her hand and fled and got out of the house. And as soon as she saw that he had left his garment in her hand and had fled out of the house, she called to the men of her household and said to them, "See, he has brought among us a Hebrew to laugh at us. He came in to me to lie with me, and I cried out with a loud voice. And as soon as he heard that I lifted up my voice and cried out, he left his garment beside me and fled and got out of the house." Then she laid up his garment by her until his master came home, and she told him the same story.

–Genesis 39:7-17

As soon as his master heard the words that his wife spoke to him, "This is the way your servant treated me," his anger was kindled. And Joseph's master took him and put him into the prison, the place where the king's prisoners were confined, and he was there in prison. But the LORD was with Joseph and showed him steadfast love and gave him favor in the sight of the keeper of the prison. And the keeper of the prison put Joseph in charge of all the prisoners who were in the prison. Whatever was done there, he was the one who did it. The keeper of the prison paid no attention to anything that was in Joseph's charge, because the LORD was with him. And whatever he did, the LORD made it succeed.

–Genesis 39:19-23

Some time after this, the cupbearer of the king of Egypt and his baker committed an offense against their lord the king of Egypt. And Pharaoh was angry with his two officers, the chief cupbearer and the chief baker, and he put them in custody in the house of the captain of the guard, in the prison where Joseph was confined. The captain of the guard appointed Joseph to be with them, and he attended them. They continued for some time in custody. And one night they both dreamed—the cupbearer and the baker of the king of Egypt, who were confined in the prison—each his own dream, and each dream with its own interpretation. When Joseph came to them in the morning, he saw that they were troubled. So he asked Pharaoh's officers who were with him in custody in his master's house, "Why are your faces downcast today?" They said to him, "We have had dreams, and there is no one to interpret them." And Joseph said to them, "Do not interpretations belong to God? Please tell them to me."

So the chief cupbearer told his dream to Joseph and said to him, "In my dream there was a vine before me, and on the vine there were three branches. As soon as it budded, its blossoms shot forth, and the clusters ripened into grapes. Pharaoh's cup was in my hand, and I took the grapes and pressed them into Pharaoh's cup and placed the cup in Pharaoh's hand." Then Joseph said to him, "This is its interpretation: the three branches are three days. In three days Pharaoh will lift up your head and restore you to your office, and you shall place Pharaoh's cup in his hand as formerly, when you were his cupbearer. Only remember me, when it is well with you, and please do me the kindness to mention me to Pharaoh, and so get me out of this house. For I was indeed stolen out of the land of the Hebrews, and here also I have done nothing that they should put me into the pit."

When the chief baker saw that the interpretation was favorable, he said to Joseph, "I also had a dream: there were three cake baskets on my head, and in the uppermost basket there were all sorts of baked food for Pharaoh, but the birds were eating it out of the basket on my head." And Joseph answered and said, "This is its interpretation: the three baskets are three days. In three days Pharaoh will lift up your head—from you!—and hang you on a tree. And the birds will eat the flesh from you."

On the third day, which was Pharaoh's birthday, he made a feast for all his servants and lifted up the head of the chief cupbearer and the head of the chief baker among his servants. He restored the chief cupbearer to his position, and he placed the cup in Pharaoh's hand. But he hanged the chief baker, as Joseph had interpreted to them. Yet the chief cupbearer did not remember Joseph, but forgot him.

–Genesis 40:1-23

After two whole years, Pharaoh dreamed . . . And Pharaoh awoke. And he fell asleep and dreamed a second time. . . . And Pharaoh woke, and behold, it was a dream. So in the morning his spirit was troubled, and he sent and called for all the magicians of Egypt and all its wise men. Pharaoh told them his dreams, but there was none who could interpret them to Pharaoh.

–Genesis 41:1, 4-5, 7-8

Then the chief cupbearer said to Pharaoh, "I remember my offenses today. When Pharaoh was angry with his servants and put me and the chief baker in custody in the house of the captain of the guard, we dreamed on the same night, he and I, each having a dream with its own interpretation. A young Hebrew was there with us, a servant of the captain of the guard. When we told him, he interpreted our dreams to us, giving an interpretation to each man according to his dream. And as he interpreted to us, so it came about. I was restored to my office, and the baker was hanged."

Then Pharaoh sent and called Joseph, and they quickly brought him out of the pit. And when he had shaved himself and changed his clothes, he came in before Pharaoh. And Pharaoh said to Joseph, "I have had a dream, and there is no one who can interpret it. I have heard it said of you that when you hear a dream you can interpret it." Joseph answered Pharaoh, "It is not in me; God will give Pharaoh a favorable answer." Then Pharaoh said to Joseph, "Behold, in my dream I was standing on the banks of the Nile. Seven cows, plump and attractive, came up out of the Nile and fed in the reed grass. Seven other cows came up after them, poor and very ugly and thin, such as I had never seen in all the land of Egypt. And the thin, ugly cows ate up the first seven plump cows, but when they had eaten them no one would have known that they had eaten them, for they were still as ugly as at the beginning. Then I awoke. I also saw in my dream seven ears growing on one stalk, full and good. Seven ears, withered, thin, and blighted by the east wind, sprouted after them, and the thin ears swallowed up the seven good ears. And I told it to the magicians, but there was no one who could explain it to me."

–Genesis 41:9-24

Then Joseph said to Pharaoh, "The dreams of Pharaoh are one; God has revealed to Pharaoh what he is about to do. . . . There will come seven years of great plenty throughout all the land of Egypt, but after them there will arise seven years of famine, and all the plenty will be forgotten in the land of Egypt. The famine will consume the land, and the plenty will be unknown in the land by reason of the famine that will follow, for it will be very severe. And the doubling of Pharaoh's dream means that the thing is fixed by God, and God will shortly bring it about. Now therefore let Pharaoh select a discerning and wise man, and set him over the land of Egypt. Let Pharaoh proceed to appoint overseers over the land and take one-fifth of the produce of the land of Egypt during the seven plentiful years. And let them gather all the food of these good years that are coming and store up grain under the authority of Pharaoh for food in the cities, and let them keep it. That food shall be a reserve for the land against the seven years of famine that are to occur in the land of Egypt, so that the land may not perish through the famine."

This proposal pleased Pharaoh and all his servants. And Pharaoh said to his servants, "Can we find a man like this, in whom is the Spirit of God?" Then Pharaoh said to Joseph, "Since God has shown you all this, there is none so discerning and wise as you are. You shall be over my house, and all my people shall order themselves as you command. Only as regards the throne will I be greater than you."

–Genesis 41:25, 29-40

Sex, frame-ups, scandal, and a bum rap are all woven together in this story about Joseph.

Joseph—a favorite son of Jacob—tall, dark, and handsome—was sold by his jealous brothers into Egypt. There he became a slave, working for a big-wig named Potiphar (pronounced POT-a-fer). This head-honcho was chief guard for the ruling king, Pharaoh (pronounced FARE-o).

Joseph's personal life was unusually clean. He is one of the few characters in the Bible with no blots on his record. Not that he was sinless. No one is! But he was a godly Hebrew (Jew) who trusted in the one true God, who had revealed Himself to the patriarchs (Abraham, Isaac, and Jacob).

Also, his work was tops. He was dependable and hard-working, and showed a lot of wisdom and common sense. His boss valued him very highly.

Enter Potiphar's wife! She was bold, lustful, ruthless—you name it. One day she propositioned Joseph to go to bed with her. But he refused. He said, "I can't do it. I'd be sinning against God. And I'd also be sinning against your husband, who trusts me with running this household."

Double-Cross and the Big Frame

Day after day she tried to get him to bed, and day after day he refused. He treated her with perfect manners and deep respect. Which was the last thing she wanted. She didn't want Joseph's perfect manners and respect, she wanted Joseph! She tried every trick she knew, but Joseph was grateful to Potiphar and was a loyal and principled man. Well, the lady turned nasty.

God never promised that the Christian life would be easy or that it would be free from troubles.

One day she grabbed Joseph by the coat and said, "YOU—come to bed with me!" He squirmed out of the coat and fled, leaving her holding it. Maybe you think it was weakness for him to flee. It wasn't weakness; it was strength. The Bible says that we should flee from fleshly lusts which war against the soul (1 Peter 2:11). We should flee from fornication (sexual relations outside of marriage) (1 Corinthians 6:18). We should flee from every form of sinful temptation.

Anyway, the rejected, frustrated woman put the coat in her bedroom and then started telling a lot of lies about Joseph. She said he had tried to attack her, but that when she screamed, he took off, leaving his coat behind. The coat was there—circumstantial evidence against him.

When Potiphar came home, he believed her framed-up charge against Joseph and had him thrown into jail.

Talk about a rip-off; this was it! Joseph had lived an honest, clean-cut life, and now see what's happened to him! He's jailed on false charges. Yes, that's right. It sometimes does happen. Even believers get framed sometimes. God never promised that the Christian life would be easy or that it would be free from troubles. But He does promise that we can win spiritual victories in spite of happenings in our life.

Cream Always Rises to the Top

Joseph didn't sit down and wait for his circumstances to change. He decided that he'd live for God right there in the prison. Just as cream rises to the surface, so Joseph started rising within the ranks. Pretty soon he had a supervisory position.

Now God had given Joseph the ability to interpret dreams. Two other prisoners had dreams, and Joseph told them what their dreams meant. Things happened just as he said they would. Within three days, one prisoner, the king's butler, was released from prison and got his job back. The other one, the king's baker, was hanged.

God does promise that we can win spiritual victories in spite of happenings in our life.

Before he got out, the butler promised to remember Joseph and put in a good word for him. But he forgot. That is, until Pharaoh was upset because none of his magicians or wise men could explain two dreams that he'd had. Then the butler remembered Joseph and put in a good word for him to Pharaoh. Sure enough, Joseph was able to interpret. The dreams meant seven years of good crops, then seven years of famine. "You'd better stockpile food during the first seven years," Joseph advised, "so there won't be any shortages in the years that follow."

"Good man," said Pharaoh. "Your God is the true God. I'm putting you in charge of all the land of Egypt. You will be second in command."

And so it was. Joseph became Vice-President or Prime Minister or whatever the second highest office was. And Pharaoh gave him a beautiful Egyptian woman to be his bride.

Joseph's experience is an illustration of Romans 8:28:

> *"We know that for those who love God all things work together for good, for those who are called according to his purpose."*

A lot of things happened to Joseph that looked like disasters. But God was working behind the scenes, bringing good out of what seemed like tragedy. Because Joseph honored God, God honored him (see 1 Samuel 2:30). And he was better off at the end of the story than he had been at the beginning. That's the way it will be in eternity for those who have honored God.

CHAPTER 12 EXAM

Use the exam answer sheet at the back of the book to complete your exam.

1. **Joseph was**
   A. sinless.
   B. a godly man who trusted in the Lord.
   C. a real "chicken."

2. **Going to bed with Potiphar's wife was wrong because**
   A. she was a bold, lustful, and ruthless woman.
   B. there was too great a difference in their ages.
   C. all sex outside of marriage is wrong in God's eyes.

3. **We should flee fleshly lusts because**
   A. we might get caught and lose our reputation.
   B. these lusts war against the soul.
   C. giving in would mean losing our salvation.

4. **God has promised that Christians**
   A. will have no trouble in this life.
   B. will never be falsely accused.
   C. can have spiritual victories even when things are unfair and difficult.

5. **When Joseph was put in jail, he**
   A. decided he might as well give up.
   B. trusted God still and tried to live for Him there.
   C. stirred up trouble among the prisoners.

6. **Joseph's ability to interpret dreams came from**
   A. God.
   B. his father Jacob.
   C. the Egyptians.

7. **Joseph told the two prisoners that their dreams meant**
   A. the butler was going to be hanged.
   B. the baker would be restored to the king's favor.
   C. they would know their fate and experience it within three days.

8. God sent the two dreams to Pharaoh

A. to play a practical joke on him.

B. to show Pharaoh what He was going to do and to carry out His own purposes for Joseph.

C. to show him that his wise men needed more training.

9. God honored Joseph because

A. he was sinless.

B. he had done enough good works to save his own soul and then some.

C. he honored God.

10. Romans 8:28 says that for the Christian

A. all things work together for good.

B. everything that happens is good and enjoyable.

C. God has no set plans or purpose.

What Do You Say?

God has promised to honor those who honor Him. How can you honor Him today? Are you honoring God?

I'M BORN TO WIN

Locked-away and left to rot,
I blamed the world for the time I got.
Mad at life, I'd curse; then cry . . .
'How could you, God? Why, oh why?'
My days were marked by fits of rage,
As I fought and kicked against my cage.
My nights were marred by fit-full dreams,
As I plotted future, vengeful schemes.
Then finally one day I let God in,
When I found a book called *Born to Win*.
Unsure at first, I had my doubts,
'Til I cracked the book to check it out.
I read each chapter one-by-one—
My walk with Jesus had begun.
He took my hand and lifted me,
From the bowels of hell and set me free!
Now His word I study every day,
From the books Emmaus sends my way.
And, like the Berean's before me, too—
I search to prove each word is true.
In my cell I sit upon my bed,
And thank the Lord for my Daily Bread,
For the blood that Jesus shed for me,
And for His work on Calvary.
And now that I'm hip to Satan's lies,
I will my faith not compromise.
I'm no longer bound to death and sin,
For now I know, I'm Born to Win!

–Poem written by Louis, an inmate in Colorado.

EXAM ANSWER SHEET

BORN TO WIN

First Name: ______________________ Last Name: ______________________

Address: ____

City: ______________________ State: ________ ZIP: ____________

Emmaus Connector: (If known) ______________________________

Institution: (If applicable) ______________________________

Cell Loc'n ____________ ID # ________________

WRITE IT OUT!

These 2 additional questions will be reviewed and responded to by an Emmaus Connector.

QUESTION 1: In chapter 2, we saw three philosophies from the characters in the Good Samaritan story. Which philosophy describes your life up until the present?

QUESTION 2: What are two lessons that you learned from the thief dying next to Jesus on the cross in chapter 9?

NOW I HAVE A QUESTION You may ask any questions regarding the course material.

PRAYER REQUESTS Anything we can pray with you about?

Reviewed by ________________

BORN TO WIN — EXAM ANSWER SHEET

IMPORTANT DIRECTIONS — 1) Use a pen. 2) Completely fill the circle. 3) Erase or X any answer you wish to change. 4) Try not to make stray marks.

COURSE GRADE

Marking examples (A) ● (C) (D) — RIGHT; (X) (B✓) (C.) (D-) — WRONG

1-1. (A) (B) (C)	5. (A) (B) (C)	9. (A) (B) (C)	3. (A) (B) (C)	7. (A) (B) (C)
2. (A) (B) (C)	6. (A) (B) (C)	10. (A) (B) (C)	4. (A) (B) (C)	8. (A) (B) (C)
3. (A) (B) (C)	7. (A) (B) (C)	6-1. (A) (B) (C)	5. (A) (B) (C)	9. (A) (B) (C)
4. (A) (B) (C)	8. (A) (B) (C)	2. (A) (B) (C)	6. (A) (B) (C)	10. (A) (B) (C)
5. (A) (B) (C)	9. (A) (B) (C)	3. (A) (B) (C)	7. (A) (B) (C)	11-1. (A) (B) (C)
6. (A) (B) (C)	10. (A) (B) (C)	4. (A) (B) (C)	8. (A) (B) (C)	2. (A) (B) (C)
7. (A) (B) (C)	4-1. (A) (B) (C)	5. (A) (B) (C)	9. (A) (B) (C)	3. (A) (B) (C)
8. (A) (B) (C)	2. (A) (B) (C)	6. (A) (B) (C)	10. (A) (B) (C)	4. (A) (B) (C)
9. (A) (B) (C)	3. (A) (B) (C)	7. (A) (B) (C)	9-1. (A) (B) (C)	5. (A) (B) (C)
10. (A) (B) (C)	4. (A) (B) (C)	8. (A) (B) (C)	2. (A) (B) (C)	6. (A) (B) (C)
2-1. (A) (B) (C)	5. (A) (B) (C)	9. (A) (B) (C)	3. (A) (B) (C)	7. (A) (B) (C)
2. (A) (B) (C)	6. (A) (B) (C)	10. (A) (B) (C)	4. (A) (B) (C)	8. (A) (B) (C)
3. (A) (B) (C)	7. (A) (B) (C)	7-1. (A) (B) (C)	5. (A) (B) (C)	9. (A) (B) (C)
4. (A) (B) (C)	8. (A) (B) (C)	2. (A) (B) (C)	6. (A) (B) (C)	10. (A) (B) (C)
5. (A) (B) (C)	9. (A) (B) (C)	3. (A) (B) (C)	7. (A) (B) (C)	12-1. (A) (B) (C)
6. (A) (B) (C)	10. (A) (B) (C)	4. (A) (B) (C)	8. (A) (B) (C)	2. (A) (B) (C)
7. (A) (B) (C)	5-1. (A) (B) (C)	5. (A) (B) (C)	9. (A) (B) (C)	3. (A) (B) (C)
8. (A) (B) (C)	2. (A) (B) (C)	6. (A) (B) (C)	10. (A) (B) (C)	4. (A) (B) (C)
9. (A) (B) (C)	3. (A) (B) (C)	7. (A) (B) (C)	10-1. (A) (B) (C)	5. (A) (B) (C)
10. (A) (B) (C)	4. (A) (B) (C)	8. (A) (B) (C)	2. (A) (B) (C)	6. (A) (B) (C)
3-1. (A) (B) (C)	5. (A) (B) (C)	9. (A) (B) (C)	3. (A) (B) (C)	7. (A) (B) (C)
2. (A) (B) (C)	6. (A) (B) (C)	10. (A) (B) (C)	4. (A) (B) (C)	8. (A) (B) (C)
3. (A) (B) (C)	7. (A) (B) (C)	8-1. (A) (B) (C)	5. (A) (B) (C)	9. (A) (B) (C)
4. (A) (B) (C)	8. (A) (B) (C)	2. (A) (B) (C)	6. (A) (B) (C)	10. (A) (B) (C)

Form Identifier -- Do not mark

MY PERSONAL ANSWER

A Prayer

Lord Jesus, I realize that I am a lost, guilty, hell-deserving sinner. I believe that You, Lord Jesus, died as my Substitute, paying the penalty of my sins, and rose again from the dead. I know that I cannot be forgiven of my sins and saved from hell apart from faith in You. I now receive You, Lord Jesus Christ, as my personal Savior.

Congratulations on the completion of the twelve lessons in this course. This is a tribute to your self-discipline and seriousness of purpose.

But the real test is your response to the Gospel message, which you have been studying. In the spaces below, you have an opportunity to state exactly where you stand with regard to your soul's salvation.

Please answer the following questions by writing "Yes" or "No" in the appropriate space and return with your exams.

1. Have you ever realized yourself to be a lost, guilty sinner who deserves to go to hell? ______
2. Do you understand that the Lord Jesus Christ died as your Substitute on the cross, paying the penalty for your sins, and rose again from the dead? ______
3. Do you agree with God about your sins and realize that the only way you can be forgiven is through faith in the Lord Jesus Christ? ______
4. Do you, realizing you are a sinner, receive the Lord Jesus Christ as your personal Savior? ______

If, from your heart, you have answered "Yes" to these questions then read 1 John 5:11-13.

CONTINUED ON REVERSE SIDE

CONTINUED FROM REVERSE SIDE

Please check one only:

_______ Before enrolling in this Course, I had been born again by receiving Christ as my personal Savior.

_______ During the study of these lessons, I have received the Lord Jesus by faith.

_______ I here and now and now receive the Lord Jesus Christ as my Savior.

_______ I am definitely interested in being saved, but I would like to have additional information regarding the following subjects.

____

____

____

____

____

____

_______ I am still not saved.

EXAMS TO: JOHN PLASTERER
BCDC CHAPLAIN'S OFFICE
OR MAIL TO
BALTO SCHOOL OF BIBLE
1712 PARK AVE BALT MD 21217

Fill in your information below, and mail back this sheet with your exam answer sheet.

First Name: ____________________ Last Name: ____________________

Address: ____

City: ____________________ State: __________ ZIP: __________

Emmaus Connector: (If known) ______________________________

Institution: (If applicable) ______________________________

Cell Loc'n ______________ ID # ______________